TO DISCERN DIVINITY:

A Discussion and Interpolation of Spinoza's "Ethics"
Part 1 - Concerning God

Charles M. Saunders

Pulayana Publishing
2016

Copyright © 2016 by Charles M. Saunders

All rights reserved. This book or any portion thereof may not be reproduced or used in any manner whatsoever without the express written permission of the publisher except for the use of brief quotation in a book review or scholarly journal or pursuit.

First Printing 2016

ISBN-13: 978-0692695456

Pulayana Publishing
3864 Botticelli Street
Lake Oswego, OR 97035 USA
Email: Spinozapula1@gmail.com

About The Series 1-6

This Pamphlet is number three in a series of six Pamphlets. The series is comprised of six individual pieces called Pamphlets. Taken together they represent an extended discussion, overview and commentary on the philosophy of Baruch Spinoza.

Pamphlet 1 covers what is often referred to as Spinoza's 'Fragment'; its formal title is "On the Improvement of the Understanding" or "Emendatione Intellectus".

The remaining five pamphlets each cover one chapter or part of the "Ethics Demonstrated in Geometrical Order" or "Ethica Geometrica Demonstrata".

The reason for this grouping is to address the contention that not enough attention has been paid to an in-depth look at Spinoza's words. At the same time another two-part goal for the collection is to present Spinoza's ideas in a readily understandable format to the capable student of philosophy, and to open up a discussion on the applicability of Baruch's ideas to contemporary challenges faced by all humanity,

Perhaps if as many of us as possible will join our efforts together until we gain a momentum which will propel Baruch's elegant thoughts out into the world at large we will all together gain the capability to grasp the intended meaning of the incomparable Lewis Browne when he wrote:

"Twelve long years Spinoza had labored interrupted on [the Ethics]; but at last it was done. Not a paragraph in it but had repeatedly been revised, not a sentence but had again and again been rewritten. And now the whole thing stood there like a beautiful Greek temple, each stone in its wall accurately hewn and perfectly laid, all the columns symmetrically spaced and unshakably grounded.

"I do not claim that I have found the best Philosophy," he declared some months later. "But I know this- that I think the true one."

This then must be our goal, to consciously tap into the power and almost unlimited ability of the human mind to understand the universe and thus to sustain us and to secure humanity's place in the future.

Charles Saunders
Spring 2016

THIS PAMPHLET IS DEDICATED TO MY INSPIRATION AND DELIGHT IN LIFE

DIANE LOUISE

Axiom 3

"From a given definite cause an effect necessarily follows;
and, on the other hand,
if no definite cause be granted,
it is impossible that an effect can follow."
Ethics Part 1- Concerning God

Cause and effect; the irrevocable and undeniable coupling that forms the basis for everything that humans can comprehend about our world; and the key to understanding our place in god's nature.

CONTENTS

	PAGE
Excerpt- The Sickness unto Death, Soren Kierkegaard	7
Letter Exchange between Henry Oldenburg and Spinoza- 1661-1665	10
Preface, Pamphlet 2	13
To Discern Divinity- A Discussion and Interpolation of Spinoza's "Ethics"	17
Part 1 Concerning God, Pamphlet 2	20

A question which must be posed to and somehow addressed by each of us before we begin

Section One:
A Little Perspective and Some Human Geometry
Part 1 of the Ethics- Concerning God

Section Two:	46

Baruch Spinoza- "Ethics Demonstrated in Geometric Order"

Part 1-Concerning God, Our Work, Spinoza's Axioms	51
Closure	110
Recommended Reading	113

Excerpt: The Sickness unto Death
Soren Kierkegaard
1848

"Man is a spirit. But what is spirit? Spirit is the self. But what is the self? The self is a relation which relates itself to its own self, or it is that in the relation [which accounts for it] that the relation relates itself to its own self; the self is not the relation but [consists in the fact] that the relation relates itself to its own self. Man is a synthesis of the infinite and the finite, of the temporal and the eternal, of freedom and necessity, in short it is a synthesis. A synthesis is a relation between two factors. So regarded, man is not yet a self.

...Such a relation which relates itself to its own self (that is to say, a self) must either have constituted itself or have been constituted by another."

Whatsoever each of us may take away from the Diminutive Dane's message above, concerning human spirituality, it will behoove each of us to bear that takeaway in mind throughout our discussion of 'Part 1 - Concerning God'.

Soren has been attributed with painting a gloomy palate concerning the 'human condition'. Defining our status as not yet a completed spirit need not be viewed as a negative, it may indeed yet prove a boon. The 'tension' he brings to light between the human as animal and as spirit may serve our purpose by illuminating the difficulty involved in attempting to contemplate and to understand the infinite source and cause of all of nature including the known universe. It should be approached with a sense of humility and of our own limitations.

In the end the intuitive understanding of Spinoza's concept of god that each of us will make our own, by the endpoint of our discussion, will ultimately involve reaching some clarity on the infinite nature of the prime cause of everything that is possible in the known and as yet unknown universe as depicted by Spinoza in 'Part 1- Concerning God.'

At this stage in our human mental capacity we are extremely limited in our thinking merely by the natural boundaries of our individual existence. That boundary simply stated is that each one of us is born in ignorance of our origin and each will die alone.

Spinoza defines this level of existence as a part of … "finite after its kind" [Page 1 Part 1 Definition II]. Our human condition limits by definition everything which we contemplate.

As far as we can ascertain everything comes to be and passes away. Even our most sophisticated musings on the origins of the planets, stars, constellations, solar systems and even of the universe itself all come with the limitations of beginning, middle and end which are virtually hardwired into us.

In centuries to come human thinking will evolve and in some measure advance to where at some point the experience of god may no longer contain the inescapable sense of mystery and awe which it currently holds for us.

One thing however will always remain true; that Spinoza will be noted and remembered as the first person who ever demonstrated the capability to understand the nature of god and found a way to put it into the written word.

One last word on Soren's sadness; he declared with some certainty that each person who is born comes with an inborn affliction, a natural state which holds us captive within one of the variegated levels within the distillates of despair.

"The Sickness Unto Death' consists in everyone's inability to come to terms with our own spirituality. It exhibits itself from a mild reluctance to ponder too deeply one's own existence, a feeling of foreboding or perpetual disquiet, into a deeper condition of gnawing fear.

This most extreme case often devolves into a psychotic state which in its most extreme iteration drives a tormented spirit to commit suicide brought on by the unbearable, unrelenting and searing pain in the mind which remorselessly claws at and eventually consumes the desire to live.

For others this affliction exhibits itself in a form of denial, often resulting in an inability to sleep or a proclivity towards alcohol or drugs to forget and to relieve the pain.

This is no small matter. Denial and despair afflict nearly everyone, or so the Diminutive Dane contends.

For our purposes we must recognize the signs of this affliction and engender within ourselves the courage and the persistence to master our 'angst' and to struggle with all our might to understand and to accept what Spinoza so wisely came to discover and to preserve for us; the innate power of our 'conatus' whose harnessing will lead us towards the knowledge of the true nature of the divinity and of our place and our responsibility to persist as virtual 'children of god'.

Letter Exchange between Henry Oldenburg and Spinoza [1661-1665]

LETTER XVIII. (LXII)
Oldenburg to Spinoza

[Oldenburg rejoices at the renewal of correspondence, and alludes to the five books of the 'Ethics' which Spinoza (in a letter now lost) had announced his intention of publishing]

[Henry Oldenburg (1619-1677) was the first Secretary of the British Royal Society, London]

Our correspondence being again happily renewed, I should be unwilling to fall short of a friend's duty in the exchange of letters. I understand from your answer delivered to me on July 5, that you intend to publish your treatise in five parts. Allow me, I beg, to warn you by the sincerity of your affection for me, to not insert any passages which may seem to discourage the practice of religion and virtue; especially as nothing is more sought after in this degenerate and evil age than doctrines of the kind, which seem to give countenance to rampant vice.

However, I will not object to receiving a few copies of the said treatise. I will only ask you that, when the time arrives, they may be entrusted to a Dutch merchant living in London, who will see that they are forwarded to me. There is no need to mention that books of the kind in question have been sent to me: if they arrive safely to my keeping, I do not doubt I can conveniently dispose of some copies to my friends here and there, and can obtain a just price for them. Farewell, and when you have leisure write to

Yours most zealously,
Henry Oldenburg

London, 22 July 1675.

LETTER XIX. (LXVIII)

[Spinoza relates his journey to Amsterdam for the purpose of publishing his Ethics; he was deterred by the dissuasions of theologians and Cartesians. He hopes that Oldenburg will inform him of some of the objections to the Tractatus Theologico-Politicus, made by learned men, so that they may be answered in notes.]

Distinguished and illustrious Sir, -When I received your letter of the 22nd July, I had set out to Amsterdam for the purpose of publishing the book I had mentioned to you. While I was negotiating, a rumor gained currency that I had in the press a book concerning God, wherein I endeavored to show that there is no God. This report was believed by many. Hence certain theologians, perhaps the authors of the rumor, took occasion to complain of me before the Prince and the magistrates; moreover, the stupid Cartesians, being suspected of favoring me, endeavored to remove the aspersion by abusing everywhere my opinions and writings, a course which they still pursue. When I became aware of this through trustworthy men, who also assured me that the theologians were everywhere lying in wait for me, I determined to put off publishing till I saw how things were going, and I proposed to inform you of my intentions. But matters seem to get worse and worse, and I am still uncertain what to do.

Meanwhile I do not like to delay any longer answering your letter. I will first thank you heartily for your friendly warning, which I should be glad to have further explained, so that I may know, which are the doctrines which seem to you to be aimed against the practice of religion and virtue? If principles agree with reason, they are, I take it, also most serviceable to virtue. Further, if it be not troubling you too much I beg you to point out the passages in the Tractatus Theologico-Politicus which are objected to by the learned, for I want to illustrate that treatise with notes, and to remove if possible the prejudices conceived against it. Farewell.

Preface Pamphlet 2:
To Anticipate our Work in the Body of Part 1

A Capsule- The Self-evident Truth Concerning the Nature of God

Everything which we have so far learned from the application of the scientific method about the extended universe tends toward standing in support of Spinoza's concept of the one substance which constitutes the being of and beyond that is the cause of everything.

Beginning with the weirdly named 'big bang'; all objects in the known universe emanated from one source. This source originated in an unimaginably huge detonation which exploded from its compressed state, and transformed into all of the matter and the dark matter which taken together account for all that is visible, invisible and measureable: galaxies, constellations, solar systems, planets and people.

Each of these objects, considered individually, is comprised in some measure of concatenations of elements in the atomic table.

The chemical composition of gaseous matter present during the birth of stars and the molecular chemical structure of the cause of life forms on earth stand in direct relation. Along with similar molecular elements they further share the source of their inception; pressure and energy fueled by either fission or fusion.

The 'big bang', which for our purposes can be considered at the very least as the proximate cause of the universe, begat the matter which forms the elemental structures of heavenly bodies and all planetary life forms.

Long before it would have been conceived of as possible Baruch intuited one self-caused 'substance' which could not be conceived of as other than existent and further and which must be understood to comprise a state of infinite being.

This 'ontos' encapsulates at the functional level the twin attributes of thought and extension, plus an infinite number of other attributes which we can deduce logically but not experience directly; plus the modifications of thinking, breathing, procreation; and the creation, destruction and re-constitution of every element in the universe.

If the enormity of the size of the known universe can be somehow captured and reflected upon by the individual human mind, one thought and understanding emerges and remains inescapable.

This thought is not ephemeral or phantasmagorical; it lies in the formation and presence in the human mind of the concept which takes the form of an adequate idea. That idea is of one eternal substance; essentially this is god.

Every adequate idea exists only through its correlate, an existing object in our experience. This reflexive interaction which we live with each day comprises the source of the 'self-evident' truth. Spinoza's bequest to us lends us the ability to realize that human perception is not 'inherently flawed'. It simply needs to be recognized, embraced and developed to its fullest extent.

Further, the ability of a finite modality to encapsulate god's essence within its individuality in the form of an idea is the only proof requisite for the existence of god. Spinoza said this; "…the finite demonstrates clearly the existence of the infinite".

This fundamental understanding is ours for the taking. The time and strenuous mental energy which must be exerted to accomplish this understanding on our parts is a given and a necessity.

At the point in time when 'god's essence and existence' becomes clear in our minds, it will hit like the proverbial 'ton of bricks'. But it will feel most welcome indeed.

With Baruch's guidance we can experience and understand god.

At some point in human evolution we developed what evolved into an innate skill to see through our extended world and to grasp intuitively the essence of substance itself.

This innate capability resides in a state of potential in every person born on this planet, regardless of geography, ethnic grouping or cultural affinity.

Spinoza called this capability "Amor Dei Intellectus" or the Intellectual Love of God. We may simply refer to it as god, as we stand in awe at the immensity of life.

To Discern Divinity- A Discussion and Interpolation of Spinoza's "Ethics" Part 1 Concerning God
Pamphlet 2

A question which must be posed to and somehow addressed by each of us before we begin

This will mark the beginning of the most serious and challenging work which we will ever attempt together. In our previous discussion in Pamphlet 1 we did address some weighty matters: the operating principles and structure of the human mind and how we might begin to improve the faculty which Spinoza termed the 'Understanding'; we call it the human mind. Baruch clearly paved the way for us by carefully laying out his discovery of the mind and its natural connection to the whole of nature. And yet for each of us there stood a very challenging blockage; to somehow break away from the bondage of an ancient paradigm which has inhabited and haunted humankind from our beginnings up to the present time. This is the misconception that "human perception is inherently flawed" and requires a religious or scientific construct to establish the truth for us.

Once we have broken through and established our grounding, under Baruch's tutelage, and become cognizant of our own capability to discern the truth, we are prepared for the next step.

And as difficult as this may be to comprehend and inculcate, that struggle will in no way prepare us for the enormity of what we now face.

The question posed is this: How does anyone dare to undertake a process in which the end result is to understand God? Not to reach a faith based acceptance of God's enormity or an intellectual conception of the infinite and all of its power and endlessly changing forms and manifestations, this is not the goal. Both of these are essentially abstractions which can be taken on or removed in a moment's whimsy.

This understanding of God, if it can even possibly be achieved, will be real and fully felt in every facet of our being.

Of course Baruch has done most of the work for us in the "Ethics" Part 1- Concerning God. And yet his intended meaning is so finely nuanced that it has escaped the notice of many if not most of those who have attempted to plumb its meaning. Baruch's selection in methodology of an adaptation of the ontological proof of god's being and existence has befuddled even the finest minds that have wrestled with it. And the comparative philosophical interpretations currently available in the extant have completely missed the mark on just why Spinoza chose the framework of Euclidean geometric logic to present his case.

To reiterate, taken together, the adaptation of the argument from 'ontos' along with the selection of the geometric method has proven a formidable barrier to entry into Spinoza's explication of the nature of the divinity.

It must be made clear from the outset that there is no claim being put forward here that no human has ever understood god prior to Baruch's "Ethics". If this were the case then Baruch's work would be merely a synthetic creation of his own device. For eons, humans have correctly intuited the essence and existence of god.

But what is unique about Spinoza's work remains that he is the first and only author who has adequately captured and described in an understandable format, the essence of eternity and infinite power in the form of a being driven by an obviously displayed intelligence, which we, as human thinkers, can access and appreciate.

This would be the same intelligence which is displayed to a lesser degree through the agency of the human mind.

For even one of us to attain an adequate understanding of the words which he assembled and to grasp the meaning and significance which lies behind those words may prove nigh on to impossible; this then comprises Baruch's '...difficult and rare'.

This leads to our next question which follows from the first one: How can anyone prepare the mind for an actual firsthand encounter with what is termed 'the Almighty God*'? That is precisely what we must prepare ourselves to undertake.

There are more than likely numerous ways to prepare oneself for this extreme experience. What follows in our preliminary remarks on perspective and its attendants is simply one way to try.

[*God, god- The use of the capital G will be used within the body of our work and will follow this usage in the translation. The capitalization of the word has caused not a little confusion among commentators on the "Ethics". For our purposes it will be vital to bear in mind that Baruch's god has no personality, no human features, performs no miracles, does not stand outside of what has been created and will make no final or any other type of judgment on human foibles.

The use of the lower case g is intended to serve as a reminder to the reader that Spinoza's god is not someone to obey or to pray to.]

Section One

A Little Perspective and Some Human Geometry
Part 1 of the Ethics- Concerning God

Soon we will begin our in-depth study of one of the most seemingly impenetrable segments of any document ever written into the annals of philosophy: "The Ethics-Part 1- Concerning God", by Baruch Spinoza. The remaining four Parts, while still quite challenging, have not gained the reputation for difficulty and indecipherability as has Part 1.

Spinoza is one of the most honored and argued over philosophers in the history of thought. His writings are at the same time equally compelling and mystifying.

Although he wrote, intentionally, in a very simple and readable form of Latin, his meaning and his immense understanding of the origins and inner workings of the universe and of human nature remain as yet un-deciphered.

This is not through any lack of effort on the part of the translators and interpreters of his masterwork, but rather through the extremely rare happenstance for any one individual to possess the capability to bring into focus the proper perspective and mix of talents which would render accessible and bring to light the magnitude of Baruch's accomplishment.

And thus it appears that it has fallen to us to make the attempt; together, as a sort of communal mindset. Perhaps what one may not accomplish alone the many will achieve in unison.

Our first challenge of gaining perspective will be our first task in our preparatory work for this discussion of his 'Part 1- Concerning God'.

Most commentators on Spinoza have found themselves to be more comfortable addressing the contents of the remaining four Parts of the 'Ethics' in particular Parts 4 and 5, which comprise his exposition on human psychology. The subject matter of: the nature of the mind, of the emotions, and of human slavery to those emotions and the potential to gain a measure of control and freedom in our lives is far less daunting than what precisely constitutes the nature of divinity.

And yet Part 1 contains the major and baseline concepts on 'substance', 'attribute' and the 'modalities' which establish the linchpin for the following chapters. Without an adequate appreciation for Spinoza's unique take on the concept of god, the import of the entire work remains out of reach.

That is precisely the reason for our coming together again; to make our attempt together to transform the nearly impossible task of simplifying this nearly impregnable piece into something simple and manageable and useful.

As for the arguments concerning Baruch's work they seem to hinge on two items: Spinoza's correct placement among the philosophers of his epoch termed rationalists and what, if anything, they bear in common; and his either relationship to or departure from, the theories of human knowledge espoused throughout the history of thought and exactly how much influence he derived from those who preceded him.

Essentially we shall leave those queries and squabbles to the historians of philosophy whose concerns are rankings and relationships and influences.

We will together perform the most necessary task in all philosophical studies which is to coax the intended meaning out of the author's document on its own merits alone; we shall term this activity; 'doing philosophy'.

Thus for us there stands a more solemn responsibility than ranking and categorizing Spinoza which is to attempt to clearly understand the content and intended meaning of Baruch's writings.

And yet in point of fact most if not all of the mentioned arguments stated above require one and only one simple solution; that is to recognize Spinoza as unique and truly one of a kind among all philosophers. This is the only way to see the totality of his scope and achievement.

No one has ever captured in language the breadth and depth of the subject matter put down by this only true metaphysician in the entire history of human thought.

He bears no comparison to anyone and his use of language and logic bear little or no resemblance to anything before or after him.

In that recognition and acknowledgement lies the key to beginning to grasp his intention for us, to understand the existence and power resident in our own mind and its inherent "union with the whole of nature". This 'union' separates humans from all other animals on the planet and renders comparisons to them, particularly for scientific purposes, dull and highly inappropriate.

At any rate, so much for fun and games with history, it is time for us to pass on to our work. There is much to be accomplished and little time for us to discuss the weighty matters that await us.

Preliminaries to Approaching Part 1

Before we discuss the text itself there are some necessary preliminaries which require our attention. One, and perhaps the most challenging, stands the question of how to develop and maintain the proper perspective for positioning ourselves to grasp the magnitude of the duration of time and content Baruch brings into play, in Part 1.

Although Baruch makes no direct mention of establishing a perspective through which the reader might become enabled to entertain the durational aspect implicit in 'substance'; nevertheless its 'properties' of 'eternity' and 'infinity' both indicate stretches of longevity, distance, and volumes of mass and power which no human can consciously picture.

Besides these challenges there are a number of other important points which need to be addressed as well.

Spinoza entitled the work, "Ethica in Ordine Geometrica Demonstrata", or "Ethics Demonstrated in Geometric Order" and yet his selection of precisely these terms and in particular his choice of the geometric order of presentation has been systematically misinterpreted by those who have made the attempt.

Again this is not to place blame or to point up the shortcomings of others. It is simply the fact of the matter and must be noted and dealt with here and now because so much depends on our grasping the concept of 'human geometry' which Baruch introduced.

That which we will term 'human geometry' consists in the fact that humans are essentially geometric creatures. Our ability to perambulate through dimensions of extension [walking, running, stair climbing, sitting, standing, etc.] all hinges on our intuitive and innate ability to assess and to accurately gauge distances and to virtually triangulate our way using our bodies built in gyroscopic sensing mechanism.

We do not 'observe' ourselves triangulating distance and constantly measuring the heights and clearances of walkways and entryways using our internal geometer; but it does in fact occur for us daily.

Thus it was only natural for Spinoza to lay out his philosophy using a geometrical display and mathematically designed format. We will revisit this most important point in greater depth towards the end of Part 1.

To construct a perspective on extended duration we will visit, in brief, some of the cultures and writers of various scriptures who were most adept at framing enormous stretches of time including the mythology of the world before humans took shape here on earth.

We will spend time with the Hindu peoples, the Egyptian, African and the ancient Greek cultures.

Next, while bearing in mind Baruch's insistence that knowledge, including all mathematical constructs, and its correlate, understanding, can only occur within the inward confines of the individual human mind.

We will investigate this innate function embedded in the brain by way of a mythical re-enactment of its birth and blossoming in our ancient African forbears, in the story of 'Gift Star'.

Because, by Baruch's reckoning, nature contains the source and wellspring of all of our 'ideas' and should function as our only teacher of what is true; our responsibility consists in serving as its translator. Up to this point in time no attribution for this marvelous connectivity between humans and objects in nature exists anywhere; it remains a stillborn secret.

As a necessary consequence of the aforementioned 'union' existing between the mind and the whole of nature it becomes clear that the human mind contains and encapsulates within its framework an innate sense of geometry and trigonometry which allows us to 'immerse' ourselves into and to navigate comfortably through our environment.

The 'genius of Konigsberg' termed this sense recognition the 'subjective essential' [part of the 'synthetic a priori'] and recognized its function in defining his 'Categories'.

Humanity's ingrained mathematical sensibility self-evidently has been the wellspring and proximate cause of all the numerical sciences. Geometry has served as our window on the world and has allowed us not only to measure the extended world but also to harness its power, through our innate spatial and mechanical management talents which have spawned significant structural edifices sprung from the disciplines of civil, maritime, mechanical and electrical engineering.

And yet it must be noted and remembered that geometry and the related mathematical sciences are only tools, they have no independence beyond their service to our purposes.

They have no independent existence outside the bounds of the human mind.

To reiterate, the geometric method was a natural selection for Spinoza's "Ethics", because we are essentially a human geometer. What this means is that our minds make sense of spatial dimensions through a type of triangulation which goes unnoticed consciously.

It has been noted that our ability to negotiate walking up or down a flight of stairs is such a highly complex trigonometric process that if it were not automatic, would be virtually impossible to negotiate with conscious effort.

This rendition of the origin of mathematics stands in stark contrast to the theory which currently holds sway in most scientific circles. This is the belief that mathematics is 'the language of the universe' and that through some mysterious process this knowledge 'osmoses' its way into the human brain.

It will take patience and no small struggle for many of us to come to grips with the completely superstitious nature of this 'positivist' theory. More detail and explanation will be covered in Pamphlet 3 in which we will discuss Baruch's "Ethics Part 3- On the Nature and Origin of the Mind.

For now we will proceed with our preliminaries.

In summation, this then will be the content of our preliminary work:
- Establishing a perspective on extended space/time plus eternity and the infinite, so as to condition our sensibilities to take on the challenge of comprehending 'substance'
- Grasping the significance of 'human geometry' and its 'birth' in the existence of mathematics prior to the emergence of numerical systems while at the same time appreciating Spinoza's selection of the geometric method.

This background work will enable us to be in a position to take full advantage of the text which Baruch has so carefully prepared for us.

A Little Perspective

This part of our work will require that each of us develop and utilize the skill to grasp clearly Spinoza's concepts and their meaning through employing the framing of activated ideas, using visualization and by creating what can be termed pictographs in our minds. These should be shaped in our minds so as to enable us to 'see' the interactions among the axioms, definitions, propositions and proofs as we work through the "Ethics". To maximize on the experience of studying Baruch's philosophy each of us must internalize and force his concepts to come alive.

For the moment, if we can reflect back to Baruch's example of 'Peter' from the 'Fragment', in which Peter the person and the 'idea' of Peter are co-equivalent and in large measure exact duplicates of each other.

The 'idea' of Peter is an exact replica in our mind's image of him copied virtually and exactly from the living person. Its power as an 'idea' lies in the fact that it can be accurately conveyed to other people.

By picturing in their minds what we are transmitting in simple language concerning Peter to our friends; his look, personality, and temperament, with some mental effort and some imaginative visualization on their parts, can become captured in our friends' minds as an idea.

If we have conveyed the idea capably and our friends' ability to visualize Peter from what we have said about him is up to the task, then they will have formed an adequate idea of Peter himself. And now they have the wherewithal to 'carry' Peter to others.

And so it is with most of Baruch's philosophy. The perspective required to grasp its meaning includes this ability to form images from his words and to frame and capture them as ideas in our minds.

Let us visit an example of the challenge inherent in the ability to visualize something clearly, for not everyone is born with the innate ability to visualize. It often must be conveyed in the form of a learned behavior from a skilled instructor to a willing student.

Recognition of this missing skill set is often incorporated into entry-level writing classes for the fledging author. The instructor will create simple exercises to enable the student to visualize a scene accurately and to verbally recreate it so as to faithfully render it on paper.

One example involves requiring each student to imagine that they are entering their own bedroom and describing it out loud. They are asked to picture entering the room and moving from left to right performing a description of what is visible.

They might say that entering the room they see a long wall, without windows. Along the wall is positioned furniture consisting of a bureau, a desk and chair set and a tall lamp with a dark green shade. Moving along to the adjacent wall they will continue around the perimeter of the space until they have captured, in the form of a mental picture and verbal rendering, all that the room contains.

With some serious application and practice the non-visual person will become quite capable at visualization and building accurate pictures of whatever they are imagining; a most useful skill for any aspiring writer.

This visualization is one of the aspects of perspective that will prove indispensable for our study of Part 1 of the 'Ethics'.

For our work the ability to visualize must be expanded many fold into the most challenging aspect in forming perspective. We need to develop the ability to picture vast stretches of time and space far beyond the ken of our very limited human experience of these elements.

When we compare the meager 100 or so years of living experienced by our most aged people on earth we find that we are, so to speak, trapped within our own limited perspective of time. Compared to all that surrounds us: mountains, oceans, planets and stars, ours is an infinitesimal fleck within time's immensity. In many respects we think of our environment as being static and unchanging. This diminished perspective is not a shortcoming or malaise on our part. It allows us the freedom to take in the events in our environment at a leisurely pace.

We may have some capability to picture life; say the horrible reality of life in the trenches of World War 1, 100 years ago, from early still photographs or films; or perhaps of being one of the pioneers in a wagon train crossing the Great Plains in the late 19th century.

But as we attempt to accurately picture life back beyond that point to two or three hundred years ago most of us find great difficulty in doing so.

Move the clock back further to five or ten thousand years in the past and the honest person will admit to having almost no realistic ability to comprehend anything meaningful about life in, say, early Egypt or India or anywhere else for that matter.

In addition to the temporal aspect of perspective which is an inborn limitation on our part, we also need to factor in along with the element of time a concept of vast stretches of endless space, elongating our focus from the surface of our earth beyond the solar system and past the constellations and far off galaxies. Can any one of us admit to the ability to conceptualize the distance involved in even one light-year or the fact that the sun outstrips the size of the earth by over a million times?

Consider now that to grasp anything meaningful or helpful in our quest to understand the divinity in Baruch's Part 1, to contemplate infinity and eternal elements of the universe and, to somehow make a conscious effort to contemplate them with any sense of accuracy; the difficulty will be beyond enormous. The concept of 'substance' in and of itself, essentially beggars description and appears untranslatable into a format that can be digested and comprehended.

And what sense can we truly make of infinity? In preparing for this discussion several friends were asked for their take on these subjects. One extremely honest reply was that the thought of an endless and eternal universe is too frightening to contemplate.

A number of people admitted to feeling a need to place a beginning and ending to space and time even though that begs the question of what comes before the beginning and after the end.

This example quite nicely captures our dilemma. How does one individual human, boxed in by our limited experience of time and space, approach the notion of infinity, in any sense of real time?

This is precisely why Baruch closes his masterwork with the words, "...all things excellent are as difficult as they are rare", as he refers to the task he has been of necessity required to set before us in his 'Ethics'. Yes it is difficult, nearly impossible. But after all Spinoza laid it out for us so tackle this challenge we must.

Our most challenging aspect within the perspective frame: Extended Time to Eternity

Whatever the merits or demerits which accompany Western cultures proven ability to create the present and to forge ahead into the future, one item causes us to stand out among the other great cultures of the world. This is our complete lack of any sense of an inherent connection to our ancestors' environment and our extended past.

In most, if not all of the other world cultures, the people exhibit and revere their sense of immediacy with their surroundings and with their ancestors.

Many examples come immediately to mind: the Mexican people who on a yearly basis celebrate their revered day of the dead.

In numerous Southeast Asian and Pacific island cultures the remains of the dead actual 'reside' with the living. That is until the propitious time for burial arrives.

Each of these cultures shares with the others a deep and abiding respect for the ancestors. The same can be said for each and every of the tribes and traditions in Africa.

For members of these cultures their ancestors are a living connector that helps them to comprehend and experience life after death, thereby diminishing death's fearsome visage.

This connection goes so far that it includes the understanding and commonly accepted belief that upon dying the individual who passes on will actually 'reside' with the ancestors. This residence includes the guidance of spiritual matters among the living.

Communicating actively and seeking advice on daily matters is another prominent feature in the lives of these spiritually resonant people.

Another commonly shared understanding within these cultures consists in a deeply felt reverence held for the environment which they inhabit. Rural hunters everywhere, once a kill has been completed and in a special quiet moment of silence, thank the spirit of the animal which was taken to sustain their lives. They recognize that a part of god's creation has been sacrificed so that they might gain sustenance and thus sustain and guarantee the continuation of their family and clan.

This does not mean that the people are superstitious. Exactly the opposite is true; they are acutely conscious of the interconnected relationship which binds them with nature.

While the interpretation of the interconnectedness within life is markedly different, these interpretations remain consistent with the content of Spinoza's 'ontology'. That is everything is one, in substance and in god.

The Polynesian peoples believe that every item in their surrounding environment which includes virtually all of the flora and fauna, are peopled by spirits which must be respected and protected from any harm or disruption. For them stewardship of nature is a given condition which derives from being honored with the gift of life.

Taken together all of these belief systems afford each individual with a very real time and expanded sense of perspective, as it relates to eternity and the infinitely extended nature of reality.

But for those of us within the Western tradition any trace of these elements is absent or disappeared sometime long ago. This does not demean nor elevate us in comparison to the other cultures, but it does set us apart.

Another feature within the western tradition that is absent is any conscious feeling for the extended past. We may know something about our family histories going back a number of generations, but that is about all the sense of our history that is alive for us.

The very ancient cultures like the early Greeks, the Hindus and the Egyptians cherish their ancient written histories which include the annals and exploits of the Gods in the time before humans entered the scene. The "Iliad", the "Mahabharata", and both the Tibetan and Egyptian "Books of the Dead", all share a common feature. Included in the story lines is a depiction of eons upon eons of time extended backwards into years beyond counting.

The authors speak in vivid and evocative language of the ages when 'the Giants' ruled the Cosmos for eons and groupings of tens upon tens of thousands of years, stretching far back and away to the time of the 'Ancient and Silent Ones' whose rule predated people by veritably millions of years and reached back even further than anyone could remember to the time when only the Gods held sway over everything in their purview and command.

Ultimately these ancient scriptural traditions descend into the epoch and age of humankind, when only faint remnants of such a glorious past are still evident through a wispy trail of stardust and whiffs of ancient beings existence which still lightly clings to the atmosphere of the earth.

These ancient texts which captured those famous tales from the Upanishads and various other venerated and revered documents were crafted to place before the reader's eyes dimensions of time and space intended to leave each with a sense of awe and dumbstruck wonder at the marvels that preceded our time on earth.

All of this helped the reader to frame a perspective that would allow the transmission of the cultural knowledge imbedded in the sacred texts to, as it were, seep into the minds of each person who attempted to plumb the depths of the knowledge of those who came before.

These are all emblematic of various techniques that were developed to create a framework for understanding things which could not be grasped through the use of the common language of the day.

The upshot for all of the above is that the peoples who belong to these ancient cultures share a more or less built in sense of time as endless eternity and a sense of spirituality and reverence for their environments.

For us today there is one avenue which has recently been made available which may be able to serve as a stand-in for a cultural life which is no longer available to us.

Astro scientists who attempt to unravel the prevalent current day mysteries of the origin of the universe and of celestial formation have made available to the public, for the first time, images from what is called the Hubble observatory.

This platform which hovers high above the planet and uses an unimaginably powerful lens which captures light and converts the images into colorized photographic prints has recently captured, stored and transmitted back to the surface, images of constellations and deep space configurations of ancient gaseous plumes and amalgams of ice and rock.

These effectively re-produce events which occurred in a time period which also prefigured the epoch of humankind. In our very modern and contemporary way this affords us our very own ancient transmission of knowledge.

These images of activities absolutely unavailable to the naked eye and far older than anything within our realm of experience as with the aforementioned cultures which honor antiquity, also evoke in today's viewer a sense of awe and astonishment at what occurred; so many light years away and oh so very long ago.

The challenge which we face will be to somehow convert this amazing technological communications feat into something we can latch onto and carry with us as we approach Spinoza's 'Concerning God'.

Perhaps if each of us can sit alone, at home, and pull up the Hubble reproductions and spend whatever time it takes to slowly and carefully ponder these deep space renderings, we too can experience time gone by and gain a perspective which cannot be presented in common language.

The important takeaway here will be for each of us to find some method for bridging the distance between our contemporary experience of time and space and Spinoza's world where the divinity, along with its counter parts substance, attribute and mode are as real and as at hand as the air we breathe.

On Human Geometry and the 'More Geometrica'

Spinoza never quite directly explains his choice of the 'Geometric Method' for the "Ethics". He does address it tangentially when he requests just 'one human mind at a time,' to consider his words. This is the same request being made here, for each of us to approach Part 1 as an individual thinker who has the capability within him or herself to bring to life the propositions and the collateral statements which accompany them.

Baruch's choice of geometry was quite natural as the vehicle to convey his message to the reader. If we consider for a moment the contents of any geometrical proposition whether posited by the famed Euclid or Spinoza himself, we find the same consistent format.

Every geometric demonstration contains two distinct yet vitally integrated parts; the first is the geometric figure while the second contains the proposition itself along with the axioms, hypothesis, proofs, corollary, scholia, lemmas, notes and explanations that accompany the figure and make for the complete structure of the demonstration.

Neither the geometric figure nor the hypothesis and its supporting elements can stand alone. It is only when both pieces are considered together that a complete geometrical demonstration is displayed. The figure considered on its own shows nothing more than lines, connected at the junction of a number of angles, nothing more. It is the pictorial representation of the demonstration.

So it is with the proposition. Without the support and reciprocity of the figure the story laid out in the mathematical theorem remains essentially just words on a page. It stands as the verbal representation of the demonstration.

This is precisely why the reader is being exhorted to 'bring to life' Baruch's words.

The exact same relationship which holds for the geometrical demonstration; the partnership, so to speak, between the pictorial and verbal representations is brought to bear between Spinoza's propositions and the individual human mind that reads and absorbs them.

Without the reciprocity and engagement of the reader's mind, Baruch's geometrical formulations remain only words on a page, devoid of life or meaning.

Only an active agent in the person of each reader will bring Spinoza's meaning to light. This is exactly how he understood and intended his philosophy to be comprehended, as he said it, "one mind at a time."

This also conveys clearly what Baruch meant by the self-evident nature of the truth. That self-evidence emerges and takes shape only when the thinker inside each of us ponders what Spinoza proposes to us through the shaping of his language in Part 1.

A side by side comparison of any one geometric theorem and any one of Baruch's propositional theorems will demonstrate their similarity. Simply replace for the geometric figure in the theorem, an individual human mind and for the postulate and the remaining supporting statements in the same theorem, replace those with Spinoza's propositions and supporting statements.

The figure and the one human mind both serve the exact same purpose; they complete the demonstration.

With some introspection and serious consideration on the part of the reader it will become clear that this explanation clears up any mystery surrounding the 'Geometric Method'.

It is not magic or mystery, it is plain and simple logic. Human geometry, that is, that geometry is a natural and innate function connecting the mind and the objects in the natural world.

This reality is what makes Baruch's choice of the geometric method in the "Ethics" a natural match for conveying his message about god.

Plane geometry is a reproduction in a mathematical format of one of the primary analyzing and measuring functions of the brain.

To place an endpoint on our preliminary work and to serve as an emphatic demonstration of the origin of mathematics which was forged from within the crucible of the human mind, and much prior to the development of numbers and abstract theorems; we will now take a moment or two to reflect on our collective past.

For this illustration let us return to the history of the development of agriculture. This time we need to try our best to picture in our minds how it all began and developed into what we know today as mechanized farming, which has enabled the human project to advance in its complexity, to the megacities and modern nations in today's world.

The story typically goes like this: 'About 10,000 or so years ago the earliest seed planters and accidental casters began to notice regularities in the growing patterns of certain of their edible grains which allowed for the onset of formal agriculture coupled with safe storage facility. These two advancements allowed for the growth of hamlets into larger villages and towns which eventually burgeoned into cities.

This development is largely credited with peoples move away from hunting and gathering and over time eventually freed up the bulk of their time, which had been spent on manual farm labor and enabled the onset of the industrial age and the social and cultural developments which we enjoy today.'

Sound familiar? It should since that little capsule is about all of the time that gets spent on the subject in our elementary school studies of natural science.

But for now we need to amplify this farming miracle which came about through a marriage of human ingenuity and the natural world.

Through the use of storytelling, we will attempt to piece together the particular segments of these monumental and game changing mathematical discoveries by our very observant and capable forebears. This will further offer us the opportunity to better appreciate what is meant by human geometry.

Measurement and the First Agriculturists
The Story of 'Gift Star'

She could remember; it seemed the little voice inside her head had always spoken loudly to her. At least it seemed to be loud even though she was the only one who could hear it. Sometimes it even told her stories and gave her directions on what to look for and what to do.

Even before she could speak like her mother and her grandmother and her sisters and cousins, who would always chatter and sing little songs as they walked. She could not yet join in their chatter but she did hear the little voice.

The women and children would be out of the village almost every day. All of them walking and watching the ground amidst the tall grasses and between the stubby little trees that seemed to grow everywhere. And she would hear her little voice.

They always carried their woven baskets with them and picked and plucked at the small fruits and stems and roots that they spied on their walks. This picking and plucking provided most of their daily meal.

She could remember that even before she spoke to anyone else her little voice talked to her. It told her which growing things to pick at and to chew. Often her mother would watch her as she quickly plucked and chewed on things that none of the other women would bother with. Sometimes her mother would even grab at her and try to stop her from putting those things in her mouth. But she didn't mind, her little voice had told her that the thing she put in her mouth was alright to chew.

Before long her Aunties and sisters and cousins and even her grandmother began to trust her judgment. Each time that she would let out her little squeal of delight at some new smell and taste they would all come rushing to her to see what she had discovered and to watch to see what would happen to her as she ate something new and foreign to them.

Usually nothing unusual would occur and she would show them what she had found and how to pick the best ones. But sometimes the things she picked up and ate had the evil spirits inside them and she would become sick, sometimes immediately after swallowing or even sometimes later that same day or even late in the night.

The evil spirit would seem to grow in her belly and to climb up into her throat and make her spit out what she had swallowed. Whenever the spirit visited her at night she would wake up and feel the terrible pain in her belly that would cause her to wretch and cough up that smelly stuff that the evil had put inside of her.

But she never changed her ways. Nothing could stop her from trying new things to smell and to eat. After some time and as she grew older the other women came to trust her and they all appreciated her skill and watched and enjoyed as their daily foods grew in new types and tastes.

She also played little games in her head with the spaces between the sparsely growing scrub trees and plants. Her budding imagination helped her to draw imaginary lines from tree to tree and she even used little dots with her eyes which she used to trace lines alongside the grasses; all of this, she did silently, it was her game, her personal fun.

As a young woman before she even began to notice boys and men and what they might be all about, she would go off by herself into the open savanna that lay beyond the safe limits of the grasses and scrub trees that shielded her people from the wild things out there. And she would dream.

Out in the open lands her little voice would begin to tell her about new things. Not about things to pick at and to eat but very different things; things about making little rows on the ground and planting seeds and starts in the rows. She never asked herself why she saw these things.

As the summers grew on her, her sense of smell and sight grew alongside. She spent more time now on the fringes of the safe bushy areas and a longing began to gnaw at her budding skills to test them further out where the feral hunters and scavengers still held sway over her peoples' lives.

She knew much better than to wander out alone. Her senses warned her that she would not last for long once the animals smelled her presence among them in their kingdom.

And so she began to entreat her father to allow her to travel out with the men and older boys on the hunt. At first he merely chuckled at her girlish whimsy, but this only strengthened her resolve to join them. Her father had already been informed of her prowess and sharp insights into the women's world.

So this longing in her came across clearly to him and for reasons he could not quite fathom in himself he relented and agreed to her request.

He knew full well the challenges and dangers that awaited his as yet inexperienced and untrained daughter. Yet something compelled him to say yes to her; but only if she would agree to undergo the traditional period of training which was a life or death must for anyone who would dare to venture out.

Thus the two most difficult moons of her entire life began. She started by learning the ways to become invisible to the ravenous night dwellers on the savanna.

Any trace of her human scent was rubbed away with layers of animal feces and urine applied all over her. She became acquainted with silent movement and the quiet hand and head signals that would keep the hunting band from making any disrupting noises. She was even taught the way to cut off any cough or throat sounds that wanted to come out of her mouth by choking herself with her own grip.

She adapted quickly and soon was permitted to take part in a hunt with the men. They gave her the spirit name that would keep her safe; they called her 'Gift Star' and taught her to throw the poison tipped spear and to wield the ropes and the club used to restrain and stun the beasts.

Her permission to hunt with the men was limited to two trips only, since it was clear to all that this way would not be her path in life. She quickly agreed and after many adventures and close calls with danger, 'Gift Star' returned to her woman's world after surviving the two arduous journeys.

But what she learned on those escapades about vision and distance and safety would serve her well for her remaining years. She returned to her own world with a new wisdom and a fervent wish to find a way to help her tribe in ways as yet unknown to any of them.

Yes, many things she came to own now that had never been hers before.

One thing she would have given her heart to have missed was the knowledge of sudden, vicious and violent death.

Two of elder boy cousins, Spotted Antelope Leg and Vulture Feather, had suddenly gone from hunters to prey when the dark man eater spirit leapt from hiding and tore them viciously to pieces. None of the men could even move before the lion was upon them.

They clubbed and stabbed at it with ferocity and took its life, but not before the boys' spirits were gone.

Her father who had made the kill now wore the skin of the beast as pride and loss memory. The head was staked at the opening into the clan's village for all to see. Now those other tribes with thoughts of causing harm to her people were given fair and ample warning to stay away.

As the summers grew on her the wish that she had made grew into a plan for her people's well-being. She had begun to save seedlings and fruit tree starts in her secret place on the edge of the savanna. Her little voice now spoke loudly and very clearly to her and she knew exactly what she must do.

She found the perfect place, an opening half again the size of her village where almost no trees grew and the heavy rains drained softly away from the edges of the flat place. She cleared the small trees and grasses away from the soil and used her digging stick to turn over the dirt on itself.

As if she had been born into it she carefully paced off straight rows and placed the seedlings and fruit tree starts in two separate plots. Her keen eye for distance had taught her to leave ample room between the rows and between each tree start. She knew as the sun pulled them up from the ground that space would be needed to pass through and to pick the figs that would hang there.

The wild maize and wheat grasses were watered by the early spring rains that she had studied for those many moons while laying her plan.

It was not long before she shared her secret with the other family members and they enjoyed a bounty of food unknown to any of them ever before.

She first learned and then taught them to stack the wheat and corn and to dry the figs before storing them in roofed huts built high above the reach of the wild things.

In her later moons she watched as her village grew and the little ones lived to help in the now wide spread fields.

No one ever came to understand her secret ways but they believed in her magic and followed her ways for many years to come.

Many millennia later when this humble tribe of Abyssinian hunter/gatherers became the first Black Pharaohs of the mighty Nile delta, who gained that stature not only through their renowned prowess in battle but also in their ability to feed the masses of their tribes and the groups that joined them to form a mighty Kingdom. This was that Kingdom that spawned a Queen, that woman who would carry her people to new heights to rule two kingdoms; one Egyptian, one Roman.

This mighty union lasted until she was taken down herself by the humble asp that found the way to fell a Queen even as she slept.

Through all of this greatness no one would ever remember the little girl who listened to her voice and made everything else happen for her people through her mastery of all the growing things and by hearing that little voice.

Summary to 'Gift Star'

Almost 40 years ago, upon stumbling across a statement by Sir Thomas Heath [1861-1940], considered by many to be the truly greatest historian in the field of mathematics, which read; "…mathematics from its origination up until the time of the early Greek mathematicians did not involve any numbers"; a process of imagining just how a mathematics without numbers would originate and how it would operate began and soon, without any prompting, began to grow into a realization.

An awakening began to germinate and eventually to blossom into exactly why Spinoza selected the 'more geometrica' and why his reason must have sprung from his intuition of a faculty innate within us, a faculty which prompts its own moniker; 'human geometry'.

Hopefully the little story above will prompt within us a recognition of that sensation barely perceptible but real, not unlike invisible tentacles reaching out from inside of each of us; groping and wrapping itself around the objects in our world which surround us; tentacles which lash us firmly to our extended environment and provide us with a magnetic compass like attachment and make possible our true north and guiding star for navigating our way through life.

Not to burst any dream state bubbles; but we must now escape from this world of dreams and conjectures. We have a serious slice of reality to deal with, and not much time to do so.

Section Two

Baruch Spinoza- "Ethics Demonstrated in Geometric Order"

Part 1-Concerning God
Our Work

And so we begin. Part 1 serves as the fulcrum for everything that follows in the "Ethics". It is by far the most important chapter in the work. It may also hold the title of the most significant document ever 'penned by human hand'; that is in terms of its relevance for the continuation of the 'human project'.

What it contains is so audacious, bold, and edifying, that our attempts at interpretation may fail to capture its importance to humanity. But try we must and we will try to capture its meaning here.

Spinoza has managed to put into common language the nature, power and infinite intelligence of the universe and its wellspring and source; substance or god.

There is no persona in god. There is no purpose or plan in god. There is no one to pray to or to worship in god. There is no retribution or damnation in god.

And yet all the aspects of divinity and the awe and respect its appreciation demands put forth in all of the religions of the world, past and present, still hold true of god.

This is not paradoxical nor is it inconsistent with the true nature of what is eternal, infinite and the ultimate and only cause of everything in the known and unknown universe.

For humans the same reverence and awe struck astonishment which held sway over the lives of the prophets and all of the scriptural personalities in their belief in and worship of God, remain due to this god.

If only there were a suitable catch all term or phrase which would allow us to simply do away with the word god perhaps it might be easier to grasp Spinoza's intended meaning in Part 1. But there is no term or phrase to replace Baruch's choice of God. And so we will labor on.

And yet what Baruch has singlehandedly accomplished when grasped clearly brings this god into each person's mind and body in a new and far more approachable manner than ever before. Its appreciation will serve us well and for an inestimable length of time into the future, as we shape a new epoch in human evolution.

Enough of this, it is now the time for us to unravel this mystery by carefully examining Spinoza's words and the logical structure he employed in Part 1.

How we will proceed

As was the case in Pamphlet 1 on the 'Fragment', the reader may choose whatever translation of the text of the "Ethics" that is comfortable. Each of the translators whose work is currently available has done work which closely resembles one to the next. We will continue with the Elwes translation for consistency.

[Note- In many editions of Spinoza's writings the "Ethics" may not appear as the first work in the text. This means that the reader's version of the "Ethics" may not start on Page 1. Since this might prove bothersome in terms of following the pagination that will follow each of the italicized sections in our Work, the practical solution would be to take a pen and re-number whichever copy being used. For our Work page 1 begins with the title and the first heading which is Definitions.]

For our work we will employ the interpolation methodology in the main throughout. This means that we will be inserting data between points as per the mathematical definition of interpolation.

As was the case in Pamphlet 1 on the 'Fragment'; each participant in this discussion should at the very least complete one reading of the "Ethics- Part 1".

And further, as in Pamphlet 1, all material contained in this current work is the sole responsibility of the author. Please excuse any and all errors or omissions.

Spinoza's Definitions, Axioms and Propositions will appear in italics. They will be immediately followed by an explanation of Spinoza's words, along with bracketed notes where additional commentary or explication is required. Interpolations of various lengths and descriptions will be inserted where deemed necessary.

That pattern will be followed throughout our work.

Along with this there will be required some transliteration and some discussion as well. Feedback will be welcomed and vital for us to acquaint ourselves with one another to 'spread the word' about Baruch's masterful treatment of the divinity.

Again, apologies are here offered for any mistakes or omissions which might occur during the time we spend together. As always the reader will be the final arbiter on the worth or lack thereof in this contribution.

Most importantly, to understand Spinoza's intended meaning is not an academic or simple reading exercise. It will require mental exertion and an extensive amount of serious reflection on the part of each reader for Baruch's thoughts to come to life. It would not be inaccurate to suggest that feeling the impact and import of Baruch's meaning and internalizing this impact is part and parcel of successfully gaining a meaningful comprehension.

Only in this way will any of us be in a position to approach and to encourage others to undertake the adventure.

That is exactly why so much time was spent on the perspective section which preceded our work together. It will require an enormous stretch of each of our mental capacity to frame an adequate picture of the divinity that Spinoza presents to us here. It will not happen automatically and will more than likely take time to settle into the mind. But it will prove worth the effort.

Definition of Terms

Axiom- A maxim widely accepted on its intrinsic merit. A statement accepted as true as the basis for argument or inference.

Definition- A recursive (or inductive definition) in mathematical logic, is used to define an object in terms of itself.

Proposition- A subject for discussion or analysis. A statement that affirms or denies something. The meaning expressed in such a statement, as opposed to the way it is expressed.

Theorem- A proposition that has been or is to be proved on the basis of explicit assumptions.

Proof- A geometric proof involves writing reasoned, logical explanations that use definitions, axioms, postulates and previously proved theorems to arrive at a conclusion about a geometric statement.

Corollary- A statement that is proven true by another statement or considered to be a consequence of a statement's truth.

Hypothesis- A proposition or set of propositions, set forth as an explanation for the occurrence of some specified group of phenomena either asserted merely as a provisional conjecture or accepted as highly probable in the light of established facts.

Lemma- A 'little' theorem or a technical step in a proof.

Scholia- Annotations to the text, explanation or element for further study.

Part 1- Concerning God
Our Work
Spinoza's Axioms

1-Everything which exists, exists either in itself or in something else.

2-That which cannot be conceived through anything else must be conceived through itself.

3-From a given definite cause an effect necessarily follows; and, on the other hand, if no definite cause be granted, it is impossible that an effect can follow.

4-The knowledge of an effect depends on and involves the knowledge of a cause.

5-Things which have nothing in common cannot be understood, the one by means of the other, the conception of one does not involve the conception of the other.

6-A true idea must correspond with its' ideate or object.

7-If a thing can be conceived as non-existing, its essence does not involve existence. [Page 2]

Axioms
Transliterated Corollaries to Spinoza's Axioms

1-Discernible to human intelligence through intuitive understanding brought about by its minds' connection to the body and the body's intrinsic connection to the extended world there exists, by necessity, the knowledge of a power, intelligence, and causality that coalesces the known and unknown universe into one infinite, re-creating substance.

2-Ontologically this entity can only be the essence of a self-existent substance called god.

Lemma-Everything that exists in nature is chemically interrelated and is reconstituted in a self-perpetuating and eternal cycle, fueled by the dual actions of celestial mechanics and physics.

3-No matter how infinitesimally small or large it may be, nothing in nature [the known universe] is the cause of its own existence. [This includes Higgs Bosun]

4-For a human being the only perspective possible for ascertaining anything with certainty is self-centric [the human mind].

5-There exists an innate, intrinsic, organic and reciprocal relationship between human nature and the entire extended universe.

6-The nature of god exists necessarily and constitutes the only cause of the entire known and unknown universe.

7-The human mind and the human body commingle into a union, which forms an active representation of two of the distinct attributes of god's infinite nature, a human being.

8-A function within the human mind which has developed over an extended period of time allows any individual person to intuitively understand the cause of its own existence.

9-The finite nature of humanity represents solely through its existence, an adequate idea of the nature of infinite and eternal causality.

10-Human existence and its self contained innate thinking and bodily functions, stand alone as the only demonstration and proof required for the existence of the infinite being and existence of god.

These corollaries to Spinoza's axioms have been derived by applying the deductive reasoning methodology to the collective content of, and by amplifying the spirit consistently evidenced throughout and accumulated within, the "Ethics".

Explanation of the interrelated nature of Spinoza's Axioms and the Transliterated Corollaries

An adequate understanding of the relationships involved among causes and their effects, the correspondence between the idea as an object in nature and its ideate, a thought occurring in the human mind, and the interlocked necessity of their relationship one to another, is most easily accessed by considering all three at the molecular level simultaneously.

An example of this consists in the interrelated chemical bond that permeates throughout the entire known universe. Virtually everything in existence is comprised of one concatenation or another of every element in the periodic table.

Whether considering the birth of a galaxy, of a solar system, or of a planet from its cataclysmic formation up to and including the earliest life forms which develop and nurture future more complex organisms, they all share, at the molecular/atomic level, an interlocking chemical relationship and an origin in the physics of cosmology.

Example-Hydrogen was present and an active element in the proximate cause of the 'big bang'. It is also a constituent element in the air we breathe and the water we drink. Finally, hydrogen provides the base component for the most destructive item ever envisaged and created by man; the atomic bomb.

Hydrogen is clearly not a cause in any of these occurrences. In Baruch's parlance it is a 'modification of substance' and 'finite after its kind'.

This universe wide chemical relationship considered at the molecular level involves the commingling and bonding of base elements in an infinite variety of formations induced by enormous energy transfers. This enormous power transforms elements of what might be considered by themselves as disparate elements, through sequences of fission and fusion, into the shapes we come to recognize as the visible matter that makes the aforementioned celestial bodies and life on earth. Spinoza terms this; 'Parts within the Whole.'

Once the element of the time which is a requisite for these formations and constantly recurring reformations to occur is considered in this universe building equation; essentially vast stretches of space/time that beggar description, the enormity of the process forms a powerful impression on us, along with this comes the nascence of an intuitive recognition of some primal cause which somehow must incept these events. There simply can be no other explanation possible.

Herein resides the finely nuanced edge of Spinoza's ontological argument for god's existence; as Baruch stated so clearly:
'...humans intuited the existence of god, god did not reveal itself

to us.' We will witness together how this bears out as we proceed through Part1 of the "Ethics".

To continue our discussion; because it has been widely observed and recorded that each of these formations no matter how large or small they may be is constrained in its duration, that is, that they come to be and eventually dissipate or become re-constituted in a new birth cycle, it is clear that they are not self-caused.

Everything visible and invisible in the known universe involves a life cycle, which will eventually come to be understood to include any Higgs Bosun or any other particle, no matter how minute it may be. In a word they are not causes of life but rather effects.

The operation of all of this activity moves inexorably through a never ending process, which while not yet completely understood from a human perspective nevertheless points determinately to an overarching form of necessity. This necessity is clearly the active element in the proximate cause of everything which we have observed. There is no need to invoke any aspect of intelligent design to recognize that life on earth did not happen by accident. The cataclysmic upheaval of earth's formation, the movement of the planet's crust through the unrelenting force of plate tectonics, the acrid deathly toxic air mass which permeated the earth's atmosphere and persisted until the emergence of the most primitive life forms; all preceded and systematically formed the backdrop for the ascendance of humanity.

There is no element discernible or measurably present in these formations which can account for the vastness and apparently endless and ever ongoing process, it is truly and magnificently infinite in its expanse. The more we learn, the more does it becomes evident that there is some primal cause of this activity that we do not as yet understand.

In light of the mind stretching effort required to contemplate and to coalesce all of the information stated in the few preceding paragraphs, and to arrive at any meaningful explanation of why and how it has all come to pass, it is not inconceivable to intuitively link the requisite necessity involved in this process to an intelligent and coherent strategy.

At the same time a finely tuned distinction must be recognized.

This strategy need not be termed to involve a plan nor can it ever be said to involve a purpose or even to admit of any persona orchestrating the evolutionary development.

Nevertheless, Spinoza recognized in it a primal causality; he called it god.

For us it is vital to realize and to remember that Baruch understood all of this even before the development of the science of cosmology. And further that he accomplished this acute understanding without the aid of any deep space telescopes or probe satellites.

Spinoza used only his formidable power of reflexive knowledge and intuitive understanding, which we explored in Pamphlet 1. This near infinite capability of the human mind to comprehend nature is available to virtually every person alive, though clearly not to the level of comprehension with which Spinoza was endowed.

Baruch is the first philosopher to detect and capture its definition, as we will now experience in Definition 1. This is extremely worthy of note.

Definitions

1-By that which is self-caused, I mean that of which the essence involves existence, or that of which the nature is only conceived as existent.

2- A thing is called finite after its kind, when it can be limited by another thing of the same nature; for instance a body is called finite because we always conceive a greater body. So, also, a thought is limited by another thought, but a body is not limited by thought, nor a thought by body.

3- By substance, I mean that which is in itself, and is conceived through itself: in other words, that of which a conception can be formed independently of any other conception.

4- By attribute, I mean that which the intellect perceives as constituting the essence of substance.

5- By mode, I mean the modifications of substance, or that which exists in, and is conceived through, something other than itself.

6-By God, I mean a being absolutely infinite- that is, a substance consisting of infinite attributes, of which each expresses eternal and infinite essentiality.

Explanation- I say absolutely infinite, not infinite after its kind: for, of a thing infinite only after its kind, infinite attributes may be denied; but that which is absolutely infinite, contains in its essence whatever expresses reality, and involves no negation.

7- That thing is called free, which exists solely by the necessity of its own nature, and of which the action is determined by itself alone. On the other hand, that thing is necessary, or rather constrained, which is determined by something external to itself to a fixed and definite method of existence or action.

8- By eternity, I mean existence itself, in so far as it is conceived necessarily solely from the definition of that which is eternal.

Explanation- Existence of this kind is conceived as an eternal truth, like the essence of a thing, and, therefore, cannot be explained by means of continuance or time, though continuance may be conceived without a beginning or end.

Transliterated Definitions

1-As observed in the above explanation, everything in the known universe has been recognized to be engaged in some type of life cycle. Whatever stands above or outside of a life cycle [that is: anything which is non-contingent but rather self-caused] will also necessarily involve a function which permits it to be comprehended solely through the cognitive function of a human being, without any need to require substantiation from some external sign.

It can only be thought of as completely independent and self-existent.

2- By limited here is meant contained in or related to another thing in nature. Just as a tree, its leaves, its fruit and the roots that secure it into the earth are all interconnected and thereby 'limited' one by the other. To complete this 'growth cycle', the tree itself is interconnected to the earth. The life of any tree hinges on this interconnectedness and its cyclic nature.

The growth cycle of the tree is limited by its relationship with the earth, which grounds and interlocks with its roots and provides nutrition and water for its development.

No thought which enters into a human mind stands alone. Just as a word makes sense only when written into a sentence, and as a sentence makes sense only as a part of a paragraph and as paragraphs connected together form a complete statement or document.

This is the same relationship Spinoza uses to interconnect thoughts one to another and objects one to another. The thought and the object share no commonality; they are essentially mutually exclusive. Taken singly though one thought interconnects another thought, just as one object interconnects with another, that is, one is 'limited' by another.

3- Whatever substance is constituted of it is entirely self-contained. Because of this absolutely unique arrangement, the conception substance is effectively its own adequate definition.

When we think of the concept universe we do not add to that any other verbal construction to form a complete idea. The universe simply contains everything possible in its conceptual framework. All objects at once are conceived together when we utter the word universe. Nothing stands outside of it.

4- An attribute is the human intuitional, intellectual grasp of anything that involves substance. Attributes form the substrata of substance, and serve as the modulator and proximate cause of the modalities [finite objects in nature].

We are capable of understanding that thought (idea) standing alone and our daily experience of life (extension) standing alone are two separate and individual divisions of substance, i.e. individual and independent attributes.

5- By mode and its physical manifestation, Baruch means all of the objects which we experience in nature, in our environment. They can only be understood adequately through their reliance on substance.

We can clearly understand that the hydrogen present at the moment of the big bang and the hydrogen present in the air we breathe and the water we drink do not stand alone in our minds as hydrogen. Rather it is understood as one of the particulate and commingled elements in the earth's formation. It is to be found in every admixture present in and on the earth; its core, crust, earth and water.

Further we can clearly discern that hydrogen does not cause itself. This fact we grasp intuitively, even though we may not be able to form a picture in our minds of precisely the nature of this cause. Spinoza terms this as substance.

6-Baruch employs the terms: 'absolutely infinite', 'infinite attributes' and 'eternal and infinite essentiality' as a basket of god's properties; each one envelops into the other to form a mental image of the enormity of god's nature.

By using the term god Spinoza intends for us to grasp that we can form an idea of everything possible in the universe now and forever amalgamated in a primal causality, which is necessary and infinite. Even though we may not be able to form a clear idea of what that entity consists of.

7-Baruch now builds onto the infinite array of god's properties. By free Spinoza equates freedom with self-generated power which has no source outside of its own essential nature. A difficult concept to capture in words but which with repeated effort can be made sense of within the confines of the reader's mind.

By constrained or necessary: we can witness and at the same time marvel that even the ocean is visibly constrained by its shore line. The tides may go from high to low but will seasonally hold to a pattern. The enormity and vast volume of water and of power in terms of winds and currents which the ocean contains would make it seem impossible for it not to leap the shore line and to cover the earth.

It would not be incorrect to state that the ocean, alike in its nature to us as humans, is contained inexorably by the necessity of its own nature. It is within the nature of an ocean to hold its shoreline relatively steady and therefore to be predictable.

Necessity, it must be remarked in passing, bears no relation to determination. Determination denotes an inescapable preplanned existence whereas necessity reflects the individual aspects of the nature of the object under consideration and the natural laws which govern it.

This indicates that the ocean, under the influence of the immutable laws which govern its own nature and by Spinoza's definition of contingency, is not free but held in check by the laws of gravity and planetary rotation.

On the other hand, the influence of the universal force which is termed gravity is virtually unconstrained; its presence and influence can be detected everywhere and all at once. It is truly free.

8- By eternal, something which falls outside the bounds of time, no matter how much of duration is accumulated in a concept of everlasting and forever. Eternity contains in itself no concept of time; although all of time taken as a whole is contained completely within the mind's conception of eternity. Eternity is again, an intuitional understanding which can be appreciated and encapsulated by the mind but not framed as a common notion like, 'that which includes the sum total of all imaginable time'.

Brief for the Propositions

[Note- Spinoza's propositions must be understood in their relational aspect, one to another and the next and so on.

Often if not always, the relationship among the propositions doubles back on itself. What that means is that to understand one proposition it must be simultaneously considered by the reader's mind in juxtaposition with adjacent axioms.

For us then, the propositions are not stand alone statements nor were they intended to be taken as such. Together with the definitions and axioms, the three elements work in concert to produce what could be termed a sublime act of orchestration by Baruch.

To grasp their intended meaning requires what might be termed a sensitive balancing act performed by the reader's mind.

For our work together an endeavor will be made to group the propositions with others that bear the same relationship or which essentially complement one another.

Please bear in mind that in the end the responsibility for making sense of Baruch's formula for bringing his intended meaning to light will fall upon the shoulders of each of us as individual thinkers. This process can take much assimilation and months, if not years, of study. Let this not serve as discouragement but rather as an enticement and challenge. The reward for mastering Part 1 far exceeds the trials and tribulations involved.]

[Note 2- For the sake of brevity and hopefully clarity only Baruch's propositions and selected segments from his proofs will appear in this document. These will be followed by our interpolated statements and any commentary and discussion that will be required to flesh out the propositions.

The reader will be asked to read carefully Spinoza's ancillary statements: corollaries, notes, scholia, lemmas and explanations using a follow along method. Again, to include all of Baruch's ancillary statements would make this, our Work, unwieldy and uninviting, to say the least.

Finally, it has been noted in current scholarship on the "Ethics" that the scholia serve as a sort of substratum dialogue and invaluable running commentary which helps to illuminate the meaning of the Spinoza geometric structure.]

Propositions

Prop.1- Substance is by nature prior to its modifications. [Page-1]

Proof- This is clear from definitions 3 and 5. [Page-2]

Interpolation- Inter. - This begins the balancing act for the reader's mind mentioned above. It will be a requisite for each of us as we move back and forth among Spinoza's axioms, definitions and propositions in order to plumb their relationship and intended meaning.

Explanation of Prop.1- Those objects in human life which we experience daily: the duration of the day and our personal routine of work and leisure; all the way up to and including anything we can comprehend concerning the reach of the constellations and galaxies, are all modifications of substance. This means that substance while the necessary cause of the modes is not materially visible within our apperception.

Substance operates on a variety of levels but for this segment we will focus on its role as the source of every aspect within the real world of experience, and of every intellectual concept about that world which is conceivable for the human mind.

With the all-encompassing nature of substance, it needs have been the case that both extension and thought existed prior to human life on earth and will continue long after we are gone, along with an innumerable set of other infinite attributes which can be deduced by the human mind, but not experienced directly. [Remember- god is interchangeable with substance and substance consists in infinite attributes. Def- 6]

We participate in substance through our immediate experience of these two of its attributes, through the medium of attributes' modifications. This experience allows us to see through the attributes, so to speak, to an intuitive understanding of eternal substance, which on earth we term god or nature.

Substance is not a logical construct or concept. It is the interconnecting and necessary primal cause of everything that is possible in the known and unknown universe.

At a microcosmic level substance is further an 'a priori' construct within each individual human mind. It needs must be 'discovered' by each person, one individual at a time. It is not a given, as the mind develops and grows in its 'conatus', so does its capacity to entertain an intellectual appreciation of substance.

As for modes or modifications of substance; if we consider the over 2 billion stars which comprise our galaxy, no matter what their age, even if measured in light years, they all were formed from some gaseous amalgam, whose origin as yet remains unknown to us. This makes them, the gaseous formations and the stars, modifications, not self-caused entities.

Prop.2- Two substances, whose attributes are different, have nothing in common. [Page-2]

Prop.3- Things which have nothing in common cannot be one the cause of the other. [Page-3]

Prop.-4- Two or more distinct things are distinguished one from the other, either by the difference of the attributes of the substances, or by the difference of their modifications. [Page-3]

Explanation- First it is important to note that with these three propositions Spinoza is not presenting anything which actually has existence, he is using these three non-existent entities as an indirect method of explication to point back to and to describe the very difficult concept to comprehend, the reality of substance.

We can term this method of exposition as reflective in its form and reflexive in the action between the non-existent and the existent, i.e. substance.

[Note- To use the non-existent to explain what actually exists will appear, at first glance, to be an awkward if not contradictory formulation. There is a very solid reason for this usage and it has arisen as a response and offered as a contravention against the prevailing belief originated during Spinoza's time that somehow we must delineate between those things that are real and those things which were judged to be unreal. The properties of something real were formulated purely from an arbitrary judgment and simply stated hold that only what is measureable is to be considered as real, under this stipulation then the following items are deemed unreal: color, ideas, emotions, sensations and god. This indicates that they are not fit for scientific consideration. Fortunately for us, Baruch did not fall prey to this abominable affliction.]

For our work together we will insist on following Baruch's lead. To have any hope of ever coming to any form of adequate understanding of god, the indirect, reflexive method will prove invaluable.

Prop. 5- There cannot exist in the universe two or more substances having the same nature or attribute. [Page 3]

Prop. 6- One substance cannot be produced by another substance. [Page 3]

Prop. 7- Existence belongs to the nature of substance. [Page 4]

Prop. 8- Every substance is necessarily infinite. [Page 4]

Explanation-Propositions 5-8 form a tight band around the concept and essence of 'substance'.

Prop. 5- There can simply not be two substances, because substance involves, by definition, everything in the expanded universe. It cannot have a twin.

Prop. 6- Substance does not inter mingle it is not some fragment of anything else. Nothing else imaginable incorporates within itself the power of eternal re-creation.

Prop. 7- Again by definition of essence; that which can be understood without reference to any other thing, the idea of substance comes bundled with the undeniable fact of its existence. If we are capable of contemplating this arrangement including exactly what Baruch means by a perfect (or complete) definition, *["A definition, if it is to be called perfect, must explain the inmost essence of a thing, and must take care not to substitute for this any of its properties."* TIE Page- 35], then our mind's eye can see the essence of substance and that its existence adheres, as it were, to its essence.

Prop. 8- To complete the bundling of substance one more item must be including for it to actually be the cause of all attribute and modality, it must be infinite. Once again, bear in mind, the adequate idea of infinity does not include any sense of duration.

[Note- With the grouping of these four propositions together their relationship and our methodology [interpolation- inserting data between Spinoza's points] should be starting to become clear.

In order to begin to understand what exactly Spinoza means by substance it will be necessary to reflect both on the individual meaning of each proposition and more importantly how they interrelate to form an adequate mental image of just what constitutes substance.

And yet it should be noted that substance remains indeed a strange conceptual item. To posit something that is the cause of everything else possible in the universe, while at the same time insisting that it is the cause of itself and further has no observable presence in any object and can only be grasped indirectly through the mind's intuition can certainly be viewed as problematic for anyone to comprehend.

The term substance has always been with us throughout the history of ideas and has served the purpose of attempting to capture in a single word something which is difficult to speak about or to clearly comprehend.

Baruch chose it quite consciously to serve as the bedrock of his entire ontological metaphysical structure. As such, it is up to each of us to struggle to capture his usage and intended meaning.

Epicurus defined the universe as infinite and eternal over 2,300 years ago and made clear that within its vastness and lack of any possibility of 'center' or 'place of origin' or any central locale that there can be no such thing as a personal God even remotely possible who watches over and controls events on earth. There is, in point of fact, no 'place' for God.

If then there is no person or purpose in god, some might say that there now remains no need to speak of any type of god or 'substance' whatsoever.

So the question must arise; why did Spinoza begin his "Ethics" with a book chapter entitled "Concerning God"? If there is no one to pray to or to ask for intercession, why bother pushing the point?

Is it not enough to watch as the ancient world religions, once so vital for the development of human self awareness, begin to crumble away as one by one people realize that we are on our own and that that is completely acceptable?

The answer is that Spinoza has captured the true nature of god as substance in the magnitude and incomparable beauty of the totality of creation and placed before each human mind a concept so lofty in its content that it requires our undivided attention and our total respect. Substance remains alive and functioning as a necessary cause in each of us. To be capable of grasping this significance and of internalizing its relevance in our lives may be the task of a life time, but the reward will help us to achieve the next step forward in human evolution. So let us struggle on together.

Our next question must then become; what proof is there of this god's existence and how must we approach our understanding of 'the cause of itself' to make it relevant in our lives?

The answer to this is strange and more than a bit bewildering at first because, in fact, we humans and our 'conatus' that is our striving to sustain ourselves both as individuals and as a community; this coupled with our innate cognitive function termed 'natural light of reason' or 'guided intelligence' are the beginnings of the proof of the existence of an intelligent and a methodology of universal procreation, maintenance and regeneration.

What Spinoza recognized in his own intelligence and ability to contemplate the nature of god's essence, was that that capability, in and of itself, indicated that our adequate ideas must be sourced in the divine intelligence which brought virtually everything to life.

At some point he realized that what he was thinking about the extent of the universe and the cause of the shaping of the world around him were not the products of his imagination.

He saw that they were a mirror of what is really out there in space and time. What his mind was experiencing was a mirroring effect; an exact duplicate of everything in god's creation.

At some point following that experience the "Ethics" began.

In other words, because our ideas, when clearly and distinctly understood, must always have as their source, an entity from which an image in our minds is formulated, then those ideas can only come from something everlasting and eternal and real.

Please do not immediately balk or scoff at this. Yes, it is strange and decidedly new. Further it represents a twist on the aforementioned and oft discredited ontological proof of god's existence. Well so be it.

No arm twisting or grating insistence will be plied here. Besides which only the individual reader can accurately assess whether this description bears merit or not. Consider it carefully and then decide.

And so, to continue:

The human mind contains within the wellspring which can potentially open us to the experience of 'Amor Dei Intellectus', the 'intellectual love of god'; that sensation felt when the human mind contemplates and recognizes the enormous power inherent in the world and grasps intuitively that the cause of the grandeur and of the wonder of the millions of years of human existence and the multi-billion years existence of everything else, can be no other than that which is the 'cause of itself'

The human mind stands as the demonstration and only proof necessary for the existence of god. Spinoza said this. This is extremely worthy of note.

Meanwhile and until we accept and take ownership of our minds, the brain soldiers on and struggles mightily, a victim to the flux and vicissitudes of our own emotions and externally driven behaviors. It's high time we give it a rest and move on.

For some elucidation on this innate power in the 'natural light of reason' let us visit for a moment with the Parisian scholar of immanence and expression, who cast his light on a multiplicity of topics in the realm of ideas.

He put it this way in his explanation of how 'attribute' touched human understanding:

"If the attribute [the substrate of substance] necessarily relates to the intellect, this is not because it resides in the intellect, but because it is expressive and because what it expresses necessarily implies an intellect that "perceives" it. The essence that is expressed is an unlimited, infinite quality."

For our purposes let us transliterate and expand on this:

At some point in human evolution the mechanical brain felt its inadequacy to comprehend adequately the means for survival in the difficult and evolving terrain of its everyday environment.

Through a function which was innate but as yet untapped, the cognitive element within us harnessed the capacity to capture, analyze, synthesize and to evaluate its point of convergence with the extended world as never before. The emergence of this process, reflective knowledge coupled with an intuitive understanding opened a never before horizon onto human's threshold of being and the human mind emerged.

This was not natural selection in action or any genetic alteration. It was new, distinct, an amalgam of where human experience met with the attribute of thought in a purely 'a priori' setting to establish a new paradigm. One we have not as yet come consciously to grips with.

But we spoke extensively of this in our discussion of the mind in our 'Letters to No One in Particular' and now our work together concerns god and our ability to draw unlimited strength from the recognition of nature's infinite and eternal wellspring. End Note]

Prop. 9- The more reality or being a thing has the greater the number of its attributes. (Def. IV.)

Prop. 10- Each attribute of the one substance must be perceived through itself.

Prop. 11- God, or substance, consisting of infinite attributes, of which each expresses eternal and infinite essentiality, necessarily exists. [Pages 6-7]

Explanation- Prop. 9- "The more reality or being a thing has..." As an individual person we can easily recognize that each of us comes to be and then passes way; we are born, we live and then we die. We can also comprehend that the same death does not belong to the reality of the universe, it is infinite and eternal.

It can be said that we have a limited amount of 'reality or being' within our scope of existence. As we ponder just what may have caused the birth of the universe along with the birth of individual human beings, it's not difficult to recognize that this 'substance', as Spinoza terms it, must have unlimited reality and being as a part of its nature, of which it shares a piece with us.

This understanding, on our part, is not a concept. It does not consist of words or sentences or paragraphs. It is by no means an abstraction formed from some generalized notion of existence.

What it consists in is a direct cognition on the part of our minds. There is no medium which connects us to this recognition. It is immediate, direct, and completely intuitional, although not in the conventional definition of intuition as a whimsical type of guess.

Prop. 10- "Each attribute... must be perceived through itself." Just as we know how much we love babies and little animals and sunsets and summer days; without framing any thoughts around that love, but by experiencing it without any intermediary, so too is our comprehension of attribute.

We understand clearly that we think through our minds and feel through our bodies. Further we can realize that these are two distinctly different sensations. This experience appears as far afield from our everyday world wherein we perceive ourselves as one individual being; not as two distinct aspects which coincide within our lives. But with concerted effort and deep concentration we have the potential to separate our thoughts from our bodies and feel them as distinct.

Baruch is explaining to us that both of these, our sensations, are two finite parts of two distinct attributes which are only conjoined in 'substance' and that they along with an infinite number of other attributes comprise 'substance.'

Since 'attribute' comprises the essentiality of the modalities (planets, humans, oceans, etc.) it differs from 'substance' and is subsumed within it. By definition 'substance' does not consist in any modality, it is the one and only pure essence and first cause.

Prop. 11- "God... expresses eternal and infinite essentiality [and] necessarily exists."

The aforementioned modalities and the infinite attributes cannot be their own cause. The only possible cause must be something which effectively 'contains' the essence of every created item while remaining indivisible, eternal and infinite.

[Note- What Spinoza has accomplished so far with Propositions 1-11 is to resolve the age old dispute over what is termed the 'Ontological Argument for the Existence of God' which contains the 'Ontological Proof for the Existence of God'.

This consists in the argument that once the being of 'God' is properly understood it would be impossible for anyone to think of 'God' as non-existent. Most thinkers reject this as a circular argument or a tautology which effectively is also empty; it conveys no meaning, or so it is said.

The difficulty for each of us remains in the fact that no matter how many words any writer attempts to string together in the hope of clarifying Proposition 11, capturing its precise meaning lies out of reach.

The resolution to this age old nemesis lies solely within the confines of an intuitional understanding which resides only and solely within each reader's mind. Best wishes.]

Prop. 12- No attribute of substance can be conceived from which it would follow that substance can be divided.

Prop. 13- Substance absolutely infinite is indivisible.

Prop. 14- Besides God no substance can be granted or conceived.

Prop. 15- Whatever is is in God, and without God nothing can be conceived. [Pages 10-11]

Explanation- Prop. 12- Prop. 13- With all of this intense focus on substance and its attributes and modalities the time has come to answer the key question:

In what way is it possible for substance to contain an infinity of attributes and at the same time to remain undivided? And further if the modalities are finite how can they possibly be said to hold some element of the essence of substance?

For the answers we must turn to the genius of Padua and his mind-bending 'Savage Anomaly".

This contemporary philosopher has captured the heart of the dilemma perfectly and has eloquently laid out the relationship among 'substance', 'attribute' and 'mode' and precisely how they interconnect and interact. For this we are forever grateful.

It all incepts in the notion of 'Power'. Consider the power of the universe to create and continuously re-create itself. And how the earth morphed from a molten ball of fire which disgorged the raw material for our moon in an explosion of incomprehensible size and eventually resolved itself into a placid sphere and home to 7 billion beings who cannot even detect its rotation on its axis or around the sun? This is a minor example of the power rampant in the reciprocal exchange of energy in the universe.

'Substance' provides the 'cause' of this power and much more, most of which is beyond our ken.

It interconnects and interacts with both 'attribute' and 'mode' in a form of reciprocal 'vacillation of power'.

If we think in terms of sound waves or even better yet of the waves of energy produced by the solar flares at the surface of the sun, the million miles per hour winds formed as collateral, project out as bands of waves that evenly permeate all of the planets in the solar system.

Some of the material from these explosions, traveling at incomprehensible speeds, penetrates and passes through every object in its path.

Meanwhile from this same solar flare, at the atomic/molecular level, other materials deposit themselves and bond atomically with the residual elements present in the atmosphere and in the planets' crusts.

And yet any sensation for us from the bulk of the force from the sun storm passes harmlessly through the atmosphere and all humanity, virtually undetectable, (not unlike substance if it were capable of description).

So too does 'substance', through the interaction of an undetectable yet conceivable vacillation, disburse its essence into; first the 'attributes' which gather its near complete force to form an infinity of discrete and infinite attributes, like the two we experience: thought and extension.

It then essentially creates, through the action of modification, the more dense material elements which form the objects in our world, including us. (Think of modification as similar to the process of distillation interlaced with the process of atomic fusion).

The difference between the storms on the sun (which have a limited duration) and the reciprocal vacillation among, 'substance', 'attribute' and 'mode', is that their relationship and interactivity forms a never ending and infinite regenerative cycle, moving back and forth, as it were; changing in its form and function within 'attribute' and 'mode', but never altering or affecting the nature of 'substance'.

All of this must be borne in mind while remembering that as the 'Cause of Itself' Substance is not amenable to any change or alteration in form.

Now each of us must adapt all of the above description into language amenable to each reader's method of reflection and contemplation so that it may be readily absorbed and most importantly, internalized.

Please bear in mind that this demonstration is only an analogy or perhaps, better yet an approximation of the effect of substance on the attributes and modalities. It certainly is not intended to serve as a Spinozistic definition of 'substance'. Now we will move back to the explanation of the propositions.

Explanation-

Prop. 14- "Besides God no substance can be granted."

Prop. 15- "Whatever is, is in God, and without God nothing can be conceived."

Explanation-For Spinoza, the emergence of god/substance as one of a kind and the overarching and only explicable cause of everything, clearly incubated and evolved over his lifetime and came into full bloom and recognition in this Part 1 of the Ethics.

After working through all of the logical and conceptual permutations possible in the relationship of the extended and intelligible world to its cause upon which he pondered and cogitated during his lifetime, Baruch recognized that the only conclusion that was both necessarily true and logically consistent is for there to be one substance, and only one.

To cap this off Spinoza intentionally placed on display for our benefit his unshakeable conviction that all of the Propositions in Part 1 and the meaning they convey stand as self-evidently true.

This is the gauntlet he throws down to us, in effect proclaiming, "If you cannot see this as true then you must return again and again to your investigation and research on god/substance and your reflection on the subject until you grasp the truth."

As unfair and as stipulative as this may appear, in the end we must stand with Spinoza on this most salient point. The truth is self-evident!

God is the substrate of anything that we can think about and further, substance in all of its modifications: attributes, essences, existences and modes is the only subject matter for our experience and thought processes to understand and to act on.

And finally, God and Substance are co-equivalencies and completely interchangeable.

The time has come to face what can only be termed 'the million dollar question'. If as Spinoza maintains god has no human faculties: no personality, no position as judge, no oversight of human doings and neither plan nor purpose and certainly, no punishment in store for any one; is there any reason for us to believe in 'deus sive natura' at all?

If belief in god marks no appreciable difference in our lives simply because we have no hope of any form of interaction with the divinity on a day to day basis and if, in fact, there is no reason to doubt that a massive meteor might enter earth's atmosphere unannounced and smash the planet into oblivion, what does it matter if Baruch is right or wrong?

The answer, though not simple, is nevertheless vital and must be, yes, it does make an enormous difference that Spinoza is correct and that god plays an irreplaceable role in human reality and whatever future we may shape together.

The confidence that comes with the comprehension of the source of the enormous energy, and transformative power that not only shaped the infinite cosmos and continues to do so while simultaneously providing a tranquil space and environment for sentient beings to emerge and develop, can inform and impact our daily lives and give direction to our every decision.

To recognize that our capability to think and to understand is a part of the selfsame function that drove the inevitability of existence up to this point in human evolution, lends enormous credibility to our efforts to subsist and to succeed as a human race.

Every individual who is fortunate enough to discern divinity in this manner will, through the necessity of their own active conatus, emerge as a devout believer both in the power of god and the unique nature of the human being.

Every person who finds themselves in this position will never need any prompting or reminder of their responsibility to achieve the utmost possible for them in whatever walk of life they select. Each one's 'conatus' will steer this human project forward and that will be its own reward and the mark of a life well lived.

Further and contrary to the common understanding, once the anthropologic and anthropomorphic person of god is removed the result will not be chaos and rampant disregard for ethical morality, but rather an individual unshakeable understanding of the value of human life and a dedication toward serving those who came before us and those who will follow.

Yes, it requires a capability, on our part, to develop and to sustain a vast perspective on all that has come before. That is why we spent so much time in the preliminary section of this pamphlet on developing the proper perspective to approach a study of the "Ethics Part 1- Concerning God".

And it must be duly noted that this desire to comprehend 'nature' will not arise in everyone nor should it. Just as with any matter of spiritual affairs there will be those among us who feel no need or compulsion to 'discern divinity'. So be it.

This is not a proselytizing work, it is an informative one. That should prove enough on this topic, at least for now.

Prop. 16- "From the necessity of the divine nature must follow an infinite number of things in infinite ways- that is, all things which can fall within the sphere of infinite intellect."

[Page- 15]

Prop. 16- Explanation- For assistance in comprehending the massive volume which comprises, *'...an infinite number of things in infinite ways'* noted in this proposition, we have now at hand reliable estimates of quantities and volumes of a virtually unfathomable size and diversity of elements which comprise the known universe. These voluminous quantities can be employed to serve as a demonstration and illustration of precisely what Baruch means.

The following data comes to us through the accumulated knowledge gathered by numerous scientists from a variety of disciplines.

For our purposes; to offer examples which will help to elucidate and explicate Proposition 16 here is a sampling from this store of estimates from "the infinite number of things in infinite ways" which comprise our world.

Age of the Sun-	5 Billion
Total Human Lives-	108 Billion
Birds-	75,000,000
Animals-	30,000,000
Invertebrates-	1,305,250
Cells in the Body-	37 Trillion
Gallons in the Ocean	1.3 Sextillion
Galaxies-	100 Billion
Stars per Galaxy-	100 Billion
Speed of Light MPH-	671 Million

No serious scientific training should be required to extrapolate from these numbers, while at the same time bearing in mind, that the universe is now understood to be in some way infinite in itself (even though the nature of this 'infinity' is not as yet clearly defined), and to grasp the self-evident truth of Prop. 16.

This truth may be stated to be an adequate idea which has been deduced from nearly unfathomably huge numbers of 'things' that today fall within our ken accompanied by the required extrapolation necessary to arrive at a most startling conclusion.

Understanding the whole of nature is not a matter of educational level, intellectual maturity, geographic locale or any other contingency. The self-evident truth of god's divinity is readily available to any individual human who has become capable at discerning and experiencing a priori, the comprehension of Spinoza's true idea.

Case in point, Spinoza grasped this understanding of the magnitude of god's universe without the aid of any scientific measurement data. He inferred it from what he understood through Prop. 16 which demonstrate that all of this is brought about though the immensity and power of god's nature and intellect. This proposition, and for that matter each and every one of the fifteen previous and the remaining twenty propositions, are both self-evidently true and absolutely necessary. They compatibly intertwine to tell the complete story of the nature of god and our place in the world.

If this explanation of Proposition 16 and the use of the numerical quantities above helps the reader to appreciate the enormity of Spinoza's god, and its significance in our contemporary lives, then for this once a door has opened to the remaining elements in Part 1-Concerning God which we have opened together. That happened because relevant empirical data has been employed to illustrate one of Spinoza's heretofore apparently 'impenetrable' propositions.

By following Spinoza's methodology for accumulating and building chains of adequate ideas, we can work backward from proposition sixteen and retrace our steps, seeking out the relationships among each proposition until we reach back to proposition 1.

Baruch insisted that one adequately understood idea is by nature irrevocably interconnected with a multitude of other similar ideas which can also be captured by human comprehension. Let this explanation serve as a key and a guide to extrapolate and to tease out the veracity in all the rest of Part 1.

Prop. 17-"God acts solely by the laws of his own nature, and is not constrained by anyone."

Prop. 18-"God is the indwelling and not the transient cause of all things."

Prop. 19-"God, and all the attributes of god, are eternal."

Prop. 20- "The existence of god and his essence are one and the same." [Page 15, 18, 19]

Explanation- "…solely…by…own nature", "…indwelling and not transient", "…attributes…are eternal", "…existence…and…essence…are the same".

Nothing but god contains these qualities spelled out in propositions 17-20. They envelope one within another and fold out again, or better yet perhaps they blossom out to help us to build a picture in our minds which hammers home that for us god is inescapable. This is not a negative condition however. It links us and everything we know and do with god's nature.

Everything around us and about us involves some aspect of god.

It doesn't make us holy or godlike but it does mean that something about us is by definition special. That we remain in the main unaware of this special relationship between humans and god's nature provides the basis for the mystery and the near impossibility of grasping its significance. Spinoza frames the difficulty thus:

"How would it be possible, if salvation were ready to our hand, and could without great labor be found, that it should be by almost all men neglected?" [Last Page "Ethics"]

Thus far as we have proceeded through the first twenty propositions we have been exposed to the nature, the essence, the existence and the being of god or nature in its completeness.

As we move forward into the next series of propositions we will begin to examine all those things which flow from god's nature; these things all flow from the causal aspect of god's infinite and eternal power and fecundity.

Although these elements can be said to be subsumed beneath the being of god they remain nevertheless part of that which is eternal, self-contained and virtually part of god's nature.

They exist as interconnected elements in their finite kind and include the known and unknown universe, all of the galaxies and constellations and the mind and body of humanity.

Some of these aspects partake in the infinite and eternal while others make their appearance within duration and will ultimately pass away. But they coalesce to form one contiguous whole.

Prop. 21- *"All things which follow from the absolute nature of any attribute of god must always exist and be infinite, or, in other words, are eternal and infinite through the said attribute."*

Prop. 22- "Whatsoever follows from any attribute of god, in so far as it is modified by a modification, which exists necessarily and is infinite, through the said attribute, must also exist necessarily and be eternal."

Prop. 23- "Every mode which exists both necessarily and as infinite, must necessarily follow either from the absolute nature of some attribute of god, or from an attribute modified by a modification which exists necessarily, and as infinite." [Page- 19, 21]

Explanation- This would be an appropriate time in our work together to attempt to use illustration and analogy to demonstrate the intertwined relationship among substance, attribute and mode. Baruch might frown upon such an effort. He demanded that only pure definitions, along with precise axioms and correctly phrased propositions could serve the purpose of explicating the divinity.

But Baruch is no longer with us and our capability to live up to his elevated standard is heavily outdistanced by our limited ken. And so, we'll need to grant ourselves a dispensation to put forward a close approximation that might help us to grasp this most important tri-lateral relationship.

So then we shall proceed with the demonstration.

We will attempt to carry this illustration/analogy as far as possible. Its limitations having been noted above, let us still hope that it will yet provide some assistance by speaking in simple language about these three relationships and their reciprocal oscillations which are pivotal for us to try to grasp Spinoza's intended meaning.

Consider the hand held magnifying glass, the one which many of us owned as young natural science students; the one which we used to examine closely all manner of tiny wonders too miniscule for the eye to observe without amplification. We investigated insect appendages and blades of grass and variegated leaf patterns and hair follicles and fingerprints, and we saw in a new light, the fascinating nature of their complex structures.

The magnifying lens acted as our mediator permitting us to experience an entire new realm. It captured the sunlight and enhanced its power which converged on the surface of the glass to illuminate the subject matter. Without the sunlight and the glass we would have never experienced nature's wonders up close and so intimately.

Thus we arrive at our analogy segment.

For 'nature's wonders' we will let stand 'mode'; for the magnifying lens 'attribute'; and for the sun's light 'substance'. Now; how does the magnifying lens work?

A magnifying glass is a convex lens. Convex means curved outward, like the underside of a spoon or the dome of a sports stadium. It is the opposite of concave or curved inward.

A lens is a medium that allows light rays to pass through it. It effectively bends, or refracts the rays as they pass. A magnifying glass uses a convex lens because these lenses cause light rays to converge, or come together.

A magnifying glass, in effect, tricks the eye into seeing what is not there. Light rays from the object enter the glass in parallel but are refracted by the lens so that they converge as they exit, and create a "virtual image" on the retina of the viewer's eye. This image appears to be larger than the object itself because of simple geometry: the eyes trace the light rays back in straight lines to the virtual image, which is farther away from the eyes than the object is and thus makes the object appear bigger.

To continue the analogy and to refresh our memories, let us revisit Baruch's definitions 3, 4 and 5:

"By 'substance', I mean that which is in itself, and is conceived through itself."

"By 'attribute', I mean that which the intellect perceives as constituting the essence of substance."

"By 'mode', I mean the modification of substance, or that which exists in, and is conceived through, something other than itself."

Notice that both Spinoza's definitions and our illustration and analogy share the same point of origin; the human perspective, namely;

Def. 3- 'conceived'

Def. 4- 'perceives'

Def. 5- 'conceived'

Baruch uses 'is conceived' and 'intellect perceives' to establish the human perspective. Our analogy/illustration uses 'tricks the eye' and 'viewer's eye' to accomplish the same thing.

The essence of substance is only indirectly experienced by us through the tools at our disposal: the twin attributes.

The same relationship holds true between the sunlight, whose substance must be captured and converted into an image in the magnifying glass which then becomes effectively harnessed for our use.

Because both attributes; extension and thought constitute the essence of substance we virtually experience the essence of substance through them.

Our good fortune resides in our ability to harness the power of substance through the attribute of extension, and to comprehend its workings through the medium of thought which we have done unselfconsciously for millennia.

From the time when our earliest ancestors discovered and brought forth the attribute's power in the form of fire, up to our present demonstration of that same power in the light which is captured in the concave silicate material of the magnifying lens, humans' ability to conceptualize, understand and modify the form of the attributes have, working in concert, intuitively grasped the essence and power of substance and modified it to serve our purposes.

This does not involve mythology or mysticism and it is certainly not pantheism. This, our world, our experience, our past, present and future consists in our direct and absolutely unfiltered experience of reality. It encapsulates what is certain and true in everything which Spinoza has attempted to teach us about substance, attribute and mode.

The "Ethics" acts as Baruch's magnifying lens which he has graciously placed in our hand. We have only to lay our eyes onto its reflected light and through diligence and deep reflection to gain access to a world we would otherwise without great difficulty never penetrate nor understand.

Correlating Definitions- 3, 4, 5 with our: Light Source, Lens and Object Analogy/Illustration

Let us see if a simple summary will suffice to pull together Spinoza's three fulcrumal concepts and to link them virtually with the elements of our analogy/illustration.

Like the sun which is the source of the light which illuminates and activates the magnifying lens, so too, substance cannot be harnessed directly, without some type of mediator.

Substance essentially activates the attribute of extension which performs the function of the lens to produce an equivalent effect, not unlike the sun's illumination on the lens. Both the lens and the attribute serve as mediums of expression.

This adaptation achieved through the power of substance, permits the observer to 'view', as it were, the modifications of attribute in the person of the natural objects which, once magnified or 'expressed' through attribute, reveal its intricacies along with its eternal and infinite interconnected nature.

Simultaneously, extension 'reveals' to us the modalities of the objects in nature.

All three elements in our magnifying lens analogy/illustration: the sun, the glass and the object being magnified are; at their molecular and atomic component levels, infinite and eternal and manifestly necessary and true.

This same infinity and necessity holds true for their counterparts in Baruch's propositions 21, 22 and 23: attribute and mode, and our addition to complete the triad of substance.

We have thus closed the loop in our explanation of propositions- 21, 22 and 23.

Prop. 24- *"The essence of things produced by God does not involve existence."*

Prop. 25- *"God is the efficient cause not only of the existence of things, but also of their essence."*

Prop. 26- "A thing which is conditioned to act in a certain manner has necessarily been thus conditioned by God; and that which has not been conditioned by God cannot condition itself to act."

[Page- 21-22]

Explanation- Previously a variety of methods has been utilized to explain differing aspects of the intended meaning of Baruch's propositions. These include:

- Examining the propositions in counterbalance, one to another
- Comparing certain propositions with similar use of terminology
- Using analogy and illustration to amplify points within the propositions in the explanations and notes
- Citing text from well-known Spinoza commentators
- Creating simple examples to serve as real time models for the subject matter in certain propositions
- Alluding to the philosophical work of certain historical authors

This variety serves two purposes:

1-To avoid the encumbrance and wordiness of applying all of the varieties of explication available and using them in each and every proposition and instead by selectively choosing a somewhat different method for each of the groups of propositions, the reader has been offered the liberty of selecting which method best suits their individual learning style. After selecting an appropriate match each reader may then create their own examples and illustrations.

2-And together we avoid what might become a boring and repetitive methodology.

And so for this group of three propositions we will again shift our method. This time we will hone in upon the interrelation of the phrases:

'...essence of things produced',
' efficient cause',
' the existence of things,
 '...also of their essence',
' ...thing which has been conditioned to act'
"...essence of things produced..."

This phrase and the others which follow bespeak a relationship in descending order which Spinoza wishes to amplify for us. All of nature falls under the category of things produced by God. The commonality these objects share, including humans, is that they do not involve existence. That is that they are not self-reliant, they are contingent upon the act of God's creation of them.

"...efficient cause..." This term simply refers to that which brings something into being; in this case it is God. It further reflects the enduring connection which exists between the eternal [god] and the transient [people and objects]. God's presence within us not only makes us real it achieves the self-same status for every object in nature. ["Everything that is is in God..."]

"...the existence of things..." Something which cannot be its own cause logically speaking must be caused by something else. Each of us easily recognizes that not we, nor our parents nor even every pair of parents reaching all the way to the first people caused birth to incept, and yet clearly something did.

It might be posited, not incorrectly, that the commingling of the sperm and the egg release a power to cause birth which can only be attributed as the activity of essence. God's essence is thus the efficient cause of procreation.

"…also of their essence…" Here Spinoza inserts a vitally important distinction; objects may be contingent, with a determined beginning and endpoint, nevertheless they do contain within each one's individual existence a part of the essence of substance, or God. This is one of the many examples of Spinoza's use of what appears paradoxical and yet remains the only effective way to transmit this category of interrelationship. The infinite [god's nature] and the finite [human nature] coalesce within each of us.

"…thing which has been conditioned to act." A marionette comes to life and displays an uncanny likeness to human actions and behaviors in the hands of a master puppeteer. Even as the audience understands clearly that the player is actually an inanimate object.

Pardon the crude analogy but this is, in effect, how each and every of the objects in nature come to life, through the necessity of god's will.

To summarize-

24- All of nature contains a reality or essence which is a diminished state of things which are self-caused or which exhibit existence.

25- Placed together as a sum, the total of everything current in the universe, no matter how they are differentiated by kind and amount of completeness or perfection, the sum total of these things are enmeshed in the nature of God.

26- Everything which exhibits any imaginable life form whatsoever has been put in motion by God.

The following two propositions; 27 and 28 can be grouped with the preceding three and the explanation for them has been essentially already covered.

For that reason they will only be reproduced here without further comment.

Prop. 27-"A thing, which has been conditioned by God to act in a particular way, cannot render itself unconditioned."

Prop. 28-"Every individual thing, or everything which is finite and has a conditioned existence, cannot exist or be conditioned to act, unless it be conditioned for existence and action by a cause other than itself, which also is finite, and has a conditioned existence; and likewise this cause cannot in its turn exist, or be conditioned to act, unless it be conditioned for existence and action by another cause, which also is finite, and has conditioned existence, and so on to infinity." (See 'Procreation' example above)

[Page- 22, 23]

Prop. 29-*"Nothing in the universe is contingent, but all things are conditioned to exist and operate in a particular manner by the necessity of the divine nature."*[Page 24]

Explanation-If we can visualize incorporating the following terms: enveloping, enfolding, embracing, emanating, exhibiting, revealing and exuding into one inclusive action which comprises the totality of all being everywhere in the universe simultaneously; then we will have held, if even only for a moment, in our mind's eye a picture of the essence and being of the 'divine nature.'

As for its 'necessity'; just as time becomes intertwined and essentially interlocked by gravity and the energy exuded by light, (as Einstein's General Theory holds), and even as space warps back into itself inside the galactic womb of the black hole and recreates new worlds; and as both time and space dance together in a never-ending embrace which had no beginning nor will ever see its end; so it is with the 'necessity' of the ontology of god. No power which is comprehensible can alter its course of action.

Not predetermined to act, for that would connote teleology, but rather driven by the twin reciprocal movements of power's vacillation and oscillation; necessity or truth or reality for they all signify the same thing, binds all of nature together and ensures that all objects bend to its unwavering will.

God and everything which it encapsulates could not be in any way other than it is now and forever has been. And we are a part of this, on the leading edge of the evolution of all that is possible.

[Note-This, our human evolution, has nothing to do with the mechanical process termed 'natural selection'. One day it will emerge and become an accepted fact that it was, and still continues to be, 'conatus' which is the driving force and proximate cause behind the most essential of human biological, mechanical, behavioral and intellectual evolutionary developments.

Natural selection played an emphatic role in the non-human evolutionary realm of plants and animals and in some human biologic and mechanical functions, but as it refers to us as a cause in the evolutionary program it is a generalized abstraction and essentially does not even exist.

It will be a mighty struggle, at this point, to not conclude from what has been said that all things are somehow predetermined; but they are not! End Note]

And thus,"...all things are conditioned to exist and operate in a particular manner by the necessity of the divine nature."

Prop. 30-"Intellect in function (actu) finite, or in function infinite, must comprehend the attributes of God and the modifications of God, and nothing else." [Page- 25]

Explanation-..."all the philosophers whom I have read admit that God's intellect is entirely actual, and not at all potential; as they also admit that God's intellect, and God's will, and God's essence are identical..." [Page- 29]

[Note- intellect, will, essence- These three terms which Spinoza calls 'identical' must be understood as actions which incorporate god's power. They are not concepts to be analyzed whether linguistically or logically.

Whenever Baruch groups terms together whether in twos or threes and marks them as' identical' or as, 'the same thing', such as 'existence/reality; being/essence, we must be clear that they are capabilities linked to the power of god, never are they concepts or abstractions. This is extremely worthy of note.]

We are accustomed, or perhaps better stated, conditioned, to ascribe the act of thinking or intellect only to human beings. So much so that it is nearly impossible for us to frame in our imaginations what might be meant by God's intellect.

Nevertheless the concept of a world or universal intellect, whether potential, passive or active has been around since even before the time of Aristotle. The proper meaning of the concept and relevant application to the nature of the universe has been widely debated throughout the history of philosophy. Spinoza depicts 'intellect' as that which spawned human intelligence and our ability to reason out challenging obstacles and thus to problem solve.

For our purposes with proposition 30 we need to find a way to picture in our mind's eye an image of how the act of thinking and more importantly of reasoning and understanding holds the key for our identification with the mind of god.

What this amounts to is that thinking is not just some random quirky happenstance which occurred somewhere along the path of human evolution. It is an indicator which exhibits to us that just as we know that our feet are firmly planted on the earth and that we eat and breathe and love and fear and that these actions provide our link to everything on earth; so too, our ability to think and the subject matter of our thoughts link us directly with nature and god's world.

This will prove an awkward arrangement for many of us. It is difficult to conjure and more difficult to embrace and to catch its significance.

Unfortunately there is no magic formula that can whisk this comprehension into our lives. We must, each one of us alone, struggle to experience that our thoughts and our experience are twinned pairs. As with everything in Spinoza's understanding of life, we must internalize 'intellect' and experience for ourselves just how it performs as a function.

It may require a revisit of pamphlet number one in this series. Carefully read again the examples of the young woman and the apple tree and the grower of the orchard and the 'how to' manual on growing an orchard. The idea of the apple blossoming from flower to fruit and the act of understanding that process are one and the same thing. They exemplify the attributes of thought and extension. Again;

Prop. 30-"Intellect in function (actu) finite, or in function infinite, must comprehend the attributes of God and the modifications of God, and nothing else." [Page- 25]

We possess the capability to choose the most useful subject matter from our experience and to sort through its amalgam to ferret out only adequate ideas for our conceptualizing and attempting to understand the world around us.

If we discriminate carefully among our thoughts and select out those random ideas born in the imagination and discard them, we can actively select only those thoughts which accurately reflect the modifications which derive from the attributes.

Only in this way can we be certain to begin, to build, and to accumulate chains of adequate ideas which will strengthen our minds ability. And the more we accumulate then all the more will our minds mirror that of god's mind which indicates precisely the same thing as the truth of reality.

If we strictly adhere to this process, for as long as it takes, we will eventually arrive at an understanding which reflects, '...the modifications of God, and nothing else.'

Prop. 31-"The intellect in function, whether finite or infinite, as will, desire, love, etc. should be referred to as passive in nature and not to active nature."

Prop. 32-"Will cannot be called a free cause, but only a necessary cause."

Prop. 33-"Things could not have been brought into being by God in any manner or in any order different from that which has in fact obtained." [Page- 26]

Explanation- To plumb Spinoza's intended meaning we will need to delve first and somewhat deeply into the issues which have arisen in relation to how emotions translate into thoughts, then we will examine how the human psychological shortcomings, evidenced through our often quirky and uncontrollable thought processes in response to an externally sourced emotional attack, can be identified in any sense with god's intellect.

For this we will dwell on proposition 31 at length and then treat the other two propositions: 32- 33, as corollaries to 31.

Succinctly stated; '*intellect finite or infinite as will, desire, love, etc.*', describes the process whereby each of us first experiences an emotional sensation through a reaction in our bodies. As when someone writes: 'the fear twisted in her stomach like a knife', or, 'the pain in his head registered like a hammer blow swung by a very strong person.'

Almost immediately this bodily sensation transfers imperceptibly into a thought like: 'I do not know if I can tolerate this fear', or, 'I'm not sure I can pick my head up or even think at all with this migraine headache.' Thus our emotional response is only directly experienced when it oscillates from the body into the mind.

These preceding two examples are why Spinoza places emotions (affections) in the realm of ideas (intellect). The emotional response and the resultant thought occur in such a simultaneous reaction that they are essentially indistinguishable.

They are termed passive because they originate from an external source and are thus not self-originated. On the other hand, if they were internally originated, this activity would render them into a self-determined status and this would thus represent a conscious choice of the appropriate response to the given emotional stimulus. Further, due to the self- origination of the emotional impulse it would be 'understood' and termed active.

Because intellect represents one of the two attributes of god's nature which we experience and is virtually identical with its counterpart in the objects in nature, this is Baruch's rationale for declaring that he would treat human emotions just the same as any geometric demonstration and further why he displayed them in geometrical order.

As we will examine closely in Pamphlet 3, Baruch laid out his depiction of the interrelationship among the emotions beginning with the two extremes of 'love' and 'hate'.

From there he laid out all of the remaining emotions in descending order from these two fulcrumal ones.

We will discuss each of the emotions and their intermingling when we reach the "Ethics Part 3- On the Origin and Nature of the Emotions".

And so, to complete our focus on the '…intellect in function…as will, desire etc.' what exactly comprises the essence of a human emotion?

It is a signal precisely and virtually the same as the electronically produced digital signal which drives any piece of electronic equipment whether a computer, a radio, a television or any similar mechanism.

It is an oscillation picked up the vacillation of a wavelength from someone else's body or an object in nature and which then travels to a receptor inside the psychological nerve center, or, what is the same thing, the emotional structure inside the physicality of another human being. When the human mechanism transliterates this oscillation it transforms itself into a stimulus to the mind which results in a thought or idea, in the form of either pleasure or pain.

This signal is no different than those which emanate from and produce the activities in the worlds of motion and rest so aptly described and captured by Newton's Laws of Physics.

Thus the title "Ethica in Ordine Geometrica Demonstrata" became the only sensible choice for Baruch's masterpiece. This is how human psychology is linked to the intellect of the divinity.

End line Prop. 31"...*referred to as passive in nature, and not to active in nature.*"

This simply indicates that the human emotional idea or thought is not self-activated but rather is caused by an external source reflecting a stimulus first absorbed through the body then transliterated to the mind, imperceptibly.

Prop. 32-"Will, cannot be called a free cause, but only a necessary cause."

Corollary 1-"Hence it follows, first, that God does not act according to freedom of the will."

Corollary 2-"It follows, secondly, that will and intellect stand in the same relation to the nature of God as do motion, and rest, and absolutely all natural phenomena which must be conditioned by God to exist and act in a particular manner."

A massive stumbling block to understanding the nature and place of 'will' in Spinoza's philosophy has been the insistence throughout the history of ideas that somehow if 'will' exists in god or in humans it must be exercised and exercised freely, without any constraints whatsoever.

In point of fact 'will' and 'free' are considered as not only synonymous but inseparable, and this presents quite the conundrum when our minds wrestle with Spinoza's grasp of 'will's' accurate meaning.

Yes, it is true that will represents a choice, but it is not an unqualified choice. It arises in conjunction with the necessity of the nature of the person making the choice and when made consciously, it is driven by understanding.

The conditions and environment of our birthplace, the economic, educational and societal status of our families and the conditioning which shapes our reactions and our pathway through life; all these things comprise what Spinoza terms 'the necessity of a person's nature'.

It is a set of factors which encapsulates our being in a nearly inescapable bond which virtually dictates our reactions to events, and our behaviors and the choices we make in conjunction with those events. Most of us remain unaware of the nature and ramifications of this pre-conditioning.

Of course that is until we come to grips with the dissatisfying nature of this arrangement and join Spinoza on the path to human freedom.

But this will in no way alter the fact that ultimately there exists no such thing as free will.

In the case of the divine will, it is exercised, so to speak, simultaneously with god's understanding. Any activity originating through the will and intellect of god is free, not because it occurs at random, willy-nilly, so to speak but rather because it is not constrained but shaped by the innumerable host of variable and infinite causes which emanate from the essence of the divinity.

This activity of willing is viciously difficult to grasp and although it may be dissatisfying to admit it, each of us must grapple with the problem alone. No one else can 'twist the arm' so to speak and convince us of a particular interpretation of its meaning.

But rest assured just as motion and rest act solely on the basis of the laws to which all of their properties conform; so it is that the selfsame case holds for will. It acts in accordance with the physical and emotional structure and life experience of the person who applies their will, or ability to choose, in a given circumstance.

We may call it the laws which govern inherent individual human behavior.

Prop. 33-"Things could not have been brought into being by God in any manner or in any order different from that which has in fact obtained." [Page- 26]

As we approach the final four propositions in Spinoza's masterpiece on the true nature of the divinity we have arrived at a very crucial juncture.

Baruch has traced for us, very carefully and methodically, beginning from the outset with his first proposition, the nature and properties of substance.

He then carefully delineated its substrata, which is composed of the infinite attributes and finite and infinite modifications. Next he identified this substance and god as precisely one and the same thing.

Following from there he laid out everything that belongs to the nature of god and god's powers. He further described and enumerated in detail how god's existence and essence, necessity, indivisibility, infinity, intellect, will and creations all intertwine into the all-encompassing self-cause of everything possible in the universe.

With proposition thirty-three we have arrived at the point where a most crucial and irrevocable element in the structure of the universe is revealed; nothing can be any different or appear or act in some other way than what has eventuated.

The implications which arise from this 'irrevocability' have caused discomfort and not a little consternation among the commentators on Spinoza's work. The reason is simple; each person forms a different mental picture when we hear; 'in any order different'.

This phrase evokes in many of us a picture of every single detail in any given person's daily experience in life being somehow 'locked in' and unchangeable.

For others this phrase conjures a more global, generalized image, perhaps focused on events and epochs in time versus events in one human life. Something like; "when the war for independence erupted, it was due to a set of conditions that will never occur together again in any one space or time; things could not have been any different than they were. The Founding Revolutionaries had no other option available than to foment rebellion against the Crown."

Because of this variation in our takes on the nature and degree of preordination of events, that is …'in any order different', we each come away with a different understanding about whether our lives can actually have been determined somehow beforehand.

To attempt to sort out this predicament we shall look into the difference between the terms determination and necessity.

Determination and Necessity

These two terms have often been used somewhat interchangeably by translators of Baruch's philosophy and this has been the cause of great confusion.

This confusion continues up to the present day and perpetuates a gross misunderstanding which essentially performs a disservice to the earnest students of Spinoza who take to heart that Baruch believed that all human thoughts and actions are pre-determined.

It is clear that this interpretation of proposition 33 has deterred numerous potential thinkers from accessing Spinoza's system. Thus the sidebar we have taken here.

We must effectively stamp out this misleading notion here and now.

An argument has been conducted between essentially two ways of thinking: humans must either possess free will, which makes the future uncertain or, that every human life has been predetermined which effectively makes us captives in our own lives.

Simply stated; if Baruch had espoused strict determinism then he would never have produced a document called: "On the Improvement of the Understanding" which outlines his 'method' for undertaking a radical program of restructuring our conceptual framework in order to construct a better more informed lifestyle.

Nor would one part of the "Ethics" be called "Of the Power of the Understanding or, of Human Freedom". Again, he promotes a radical breakaway from our conditioned slavery to the emotions.

And finally, he would never have closed the final pages of the "Ethics" with; "...if the way I have pointed out as leading to this result [salvation] seems exceedingly hard, it may nevertheless be discovered."

These details should serve as aids in dispelling the myth of Spinoza's strict determinism.

Prop. 34-"God's power is identical with his essence."

Prop. 35-"Whatsoever we conceive to be in the power of god; necessarily exists." [Page- 30]

Explanation- Prop. 34- Activity, being and intellect all coalesce in 'Deus sive Natura'. We have borrowed the term enfolding and the act of enveloping from some of our greatest commentators on the "Ethics" to amplify this arrangement.

The twin activities of enfolding and enveloping serve admirably together to reflect the power and recombinant vitality which revolves within the scope of god's eternal nature.

In stating that god's power and essence are identical Spinoza is effectively removing any question of 'what existed before there were any creations?'

The answer by now after our lengthy discussion should be clear; there was never any time or duration prior to god's essence and existence, thus there were no prior creations.

As has been stated previously, since we clearly have, each one of us, a date of birth, an extended lifetime, and a certain day on which we will die, we have a tremendous difficulty in framing any adequate understanding of eternity which provides the backdrop for god's power and essence.

But we must not allow our limited direct experience of this unimaginable power which triggers and serves as the source of each and every function imaginable in the universe to cloud our ability to understand, in some measure, god's power and essence. They are one and the same and have always existed.

From the enormous burst of its fire misted birth down to the elegant latticing and nano-electronic exchanges of energy from molecule to molecule to the intricately and finely nuanced dance of messaging among the waving tendrils of the mitochondria within the cell structures in the biologic realm; the universe weaves an epic tale about power in every distillation imaginable.

This, my dear friends, contains and expresses god's power and essence in an everlasting format of reality. Baruch intuited all of this for us and wrote it into the chronicle of birth and passing on and never ending resurrection!

Let us always attempt to keep in focus that we, human beings, as finite modifications and as substrates of the infinite mode subsumed under the attribute of extension, are a part of 'God's power…and essence'. This makes us the children of god; properly rendered and comprehended.

One could never wish for nor receive a finer birthright!

Explanation- Prop. 35- When our conceptions are formed solely of adequate ideas, clearly and adequately conceived and consisting of accumulated chains of ideas, they accurately reflect, essentially as doppelgangers for the order and nature of objects in the universe which comprise a segment of the attribute of extension.

When we consciously grasp the significance of this arrangement and mentally trace it back to its source, we can effectively comprehend that the universe could not be arranged in any other manner than as it has eventuated and further that to conceive of it clearly means that it must be existent. Sorry but there is no other way to phrase it.

Of course this marks a degree of understanding which will be experienced intuitively, felt as 'Amor Dei Intellectus', since none of us contains the capacity within us to clearly and adequately frame this massive notion on the strength of the intellectual capacity afforded us.

But it can and will be experienced by those who apply themselves diligently and who take whatever time is required to master what Spinoza has set before us in this "Ethics Part 1- Concerning God".

Prop. 36-"There is no cause from whose nature some effect does not follow." [Page- 30]

Explanation- Cause and effect, properly understood, do not exist on the same temporal or contiguous plane. Nor do they belong to the same category; a cause, including a proximate cause, derives itself from a given attribute while an effect is a modality.

We can attribute the spurt of growth in the life cycle of any tree from seed to seedling as an admixture of sunlight, together with nutrition bearing soil and water; a process whose amalgamation we term photosynthesis, with the sun's light bearing most of the burden of causality.

The seedling and eventuating plant differs completely from and bears no resemblance in its form to its cause, the aforementioned photosynthesis. And yet even in their extreme difference in form they remain inescapably connected. We observe the results of that process, the tree, but no one has yet nor may anyone ever capture a glimpse nor found any method for measuring photosynthesis' instigation of the process.

It remains beyond observation and measurement, although we do, in fact, recognize its existence, through the process of reflective knowledge and intuitional understanding, as the cause of the growth cycle. The celebrated Welsh poet put it famously and elegantly thus:

The force that through the green fuse drives the flower
Drives my green age; that blasts the roots of trees
is my destroyer.
And I am dumb to tell the crooked rose
My youth is bent by the same wintry fever.

The force that drives the water through the rocks
Drives my red blood; that dries the mouthing streams
Turns mine to wax.
And I am dumb to mouth unto my veins
How at the mountain stream the same mouth sucks.

The hand that whirls the water in the pool
Stirs the quicksand; that ropes the blowing wind
Hauls my shroud sail.
And I am dumb to tell the hanging man
How of my clay is made the hangman's lime.

Dylan Thomas

To continue, this process runs counter to the current accounting of the relationship between cause and effect which holds sway in most scientific theory and practice; which is the stimulus/response model.

According to this behavioral, bio-medical and clinical research model, from a given external stimulus [cause] there will occur a measureable response [effect]. Also termed action/reaction the process assumes cause and effect to occur essentially simultaneously.

This proximity factor and relational immediacy inherent in this model of cause/effect virtually blinds us from recognizing the actual arrangement just described. An example would be the waste of time and resources incurred in seeking the cause for cancer in a patient's DNA. The proximate cause for most cancers occurred long before it surfaced as a marker in the DNA.

Spinoza called our misconception of cause and effect, our greatest stumbling block for recognizing the correct arrangement in the order of nature.

We must wrestle our thinking around to where we can see that cause and its effect are rarely in the same space as one another.

If we turn our attention towards conception and birth as an example of non-contiguous events, which bear the mark of cause and effect, we can clearly understand that a span of nine months separates the two events. That much is fairly straightforward. Further, they occur in a separate time and space from one another.

This is a model we can adapt for our use as we struggle to right our thinking mechanism towards the actual relationship between cause and its effect.

For those whose understanding already leans in this direction, these examples of the birth cycle of humans and the growth cycle in the plant world may serve a purpose.

Summary for proposition thirty-six - Prop. 36-"*There is no cause from whose nature some effect does not follow.*"

Cause acts as the driving factor behind its driven counterpart; the effect. Taken together they are locked into a reciprocal magnetic embrace. One cannot exist without the other.

For his example of this inseparable relationship Spinoza asked us to consider the relationship which holds between a mountain and its valley. It is impossible to conceive of the one standing alone without the other.

The material from the mountain top in the form of the admixture of rock and earth and of frozen water are driven downward through nature's immutable law of gravity to form the regolith which shapes the valley. And the shape and modulating drift of the valley floor with the ever present undulating river flow, relentlessly pulls the material away from the face of the mountain and gravitates the mass towards the sea.

And so it is that cause and effect are integral to one another. Each and every effect bespeaks a cause; herein lies the key for Baruch's claim that we as 'thinking things' comprise within us the capability to comprehend the order of nature by seeking out causes through careful observation and reflection on their effects.

In other words, the world which we experience is clearly an effect. It needs must have a cause, that is an unshakeable immutable law of nature, and the key to human knowledge.

Endpoint- "Ethics Part 1-Concerning God"

And so we find ourselves at the end point in our discussion and interpolation of Spinoza's "Ethics Part 1-Concerning God". There remains now only the need for a brief closure piece which will bring us to the end of this, our most challenging venture which we to date or ever in the future shall undertake together.

Our success will only become measured over time and by the accumulated number of those of us who grasp the significance of Spinoza's capture of and presentation in words of the true nature of the divinity.

Closure

There are some who might contend that we have traversed a great distance in the time which we have just spent together.

'After all', they might say, 'Thanks to Baruch Spinoza have we not traveled to where mighty substance, in all its divine glory, resides?'

'And, in doing so, have we not simultaneously, sought out and discovered the home of the mighty divinity?'

In some measure the answer should be, 'Yes, we have together done just that.' But let it be made abundantly clear that our time spent together will come to naught if it stands alone. Our work is only yet begun.

It is only tantamount to a blink of the eye compared to the time which will be required for each of us to spend within the crucible of our individual souls. This is the duration alone in deep contemplation and reflection which will be required if we wish our efforts to bear abundant fruit.

And that time indwelling on the mysteries of substance and its children, attribute and the modalities, will be a wastrel's empty dream space unless it is molded from the firmest foundation and built with sturdy frame from backbreaking toil.

Bear in mind, this foundation and its structure must be built so as to resound as clearly within each of us as does the sound of our own birth name. This building must be anchored into the earth through our grounding in Spinoza's ontology of 'being'.

The objects which surround us in nature and which serve as our connection to the existence and essence of god; they are the proving ground and they alone contain the self-evident truth that humans participate interactively and immediately with the order of nature. And further that this reciprocal interconnection comprises the frame through which we possess from birth the potential to conceive god clearly and distinctly.

So it must be, that with our clear understanding of this, Spinoza's 'Idea', which we must use as the only lever possible to attempt to pry asunder the gateway into the depths of his elegant 'Clear Labyrinth', we will gain entry.

Without this 'idea' being held steadfastly before the grasp of our mind's eye, the remaining work which we have done together will come to naught.

Remember well and feel within our beings, that the object, that shiny red apple, and its twin, that apple's presence in our minds, are one and the same. They are inseparable and dwell within each of us through our vibrant and vacillating and reciprocal connection with the objects in nature. Together they form the bonding of two of god's eternal and infinite attributes, inside each one of us.

They inhabit within us as divinity's gift and as the long sought after 'Holy Grail of Life'. This demonstrates beyond any doubt the reality of god's revealing itself to us; not in tongues or burning bushes or stone tablets but in our bodies and our minds.

Baruch discovered it for us and crafted it into simple language and now we must take up the nearly unbearable and yet weightless load of grasping the true understanding of god, of divinity and of ourselves.

Thus this closure encapsulates what in Baruch's closing words to us from the "Ethics" which have captured the elusive enigma that is the 'understanding' itself pronounces; …'all things excellent are as difficult as they are rare.'

He clearly recognized that no matter how much time might elapse into the future that only the very few and most dedicated of mind would reach his beloved 'salvation'. Yet he still and all has offered each and every one of us the opportunity of a lifetime. It remains up to us precisely what we will do with his magnificent legacy.
And now everything which can be said between us has been said.

Go now, and each and every be unto yourselves, alone!

The coming struggle will be mighty and painfully lonely at times. You will doubt yourself often and will labor mightily and for what will seem like an eternity until you reach the end.

You must wrestle with this angel on your own time and on your own terms. But the beauty which you will wrest from this toil, this 'Amor Dei Intellectus', awaits you.

In this treasure you will discover a peace and a satisfaction once believed to be wrought only for the gods.

Safe journey, all of the affection which my heart holds for you will travel with you.

And having said these things to you,

There remains only to say,

That I remain Yours Faithfully,

Charles M. Saunders
Lake Oswego, Oregon
February 2016

Recommended Reading

The Living Thoughts of Spinoza, Arnold Zweig

Spinoza- Practical Philosophy, Gilles DeLeuze

Spinoza, Roger Scruton

Spinoza on God, Joseph Radnor

On Spinoza, Diane Steinberg

Spinoza: Liberator of God and Man, Benjamin Decasseres

The Savage Anomaly, Antonio Negri

The Courtier and the Heretic, Matthew Stuart

Spinoza a Life, Steven Nadler

Spinoza beyond Philosophy, edited by Beth Lord

Spinoza's Revolutions in Natural Law, Andre Santos Campos

The Philosophy of Spinoza, Richard McKeon

Spinoza's Metaphysics, Edwin Curley

Expressionism in Philosophy: Spinoza, Gilles DeLeuze

Letters to No One in Particular: A Discussion and Illustration of Spinoza's 'Fragment' or "On the Improvement of the Understanding", Charles M. Saunders

www.ingramcontent.com/pod-product-compliance
Lightning Source LLC
Chambersburg PA
CBHW030223170426
43194CB00007BA/841